THE FILM DIRECTOR PREPARES

Everything you need to know before you shout 'action!'

by Jonas Grimås

THE FILM DIRECTOR PREPARES
First edition
© Jonas Grimås, 2016
www.jonasgrimas.com
Design by Åsa Höjer
Photographs by Kjell Dike and Yanna Buryak
Illustrations by Jonas Grimås
The printing of this book has been funded by a generous grant from
Anglo-Swedish Society and through a Kickstarter campaign
ISBN 978-1-5262-0168-3

You bought this book because you want to know how to be a film director.
You will find everything you need on the next page:

1 Filmmaking is never a mechanical process. It's when a group of people who have learned to trust each other come together and perform miracles.

2 Assumption is the mother of all disasters.

3 Learn to trust your instincts.

That's it really.

There is a fourth point, and you will know
what it is when you're finished reading this book.

BEFORE WE GET STARTED

Let me explain where I have come from. At the point of writing this, I have been a director for 26 years. Being a director is the best job on the planet. Since I started directing I have never worked a single day of my life: I have just been very fortunate and privileged to practice my hobby and get paid for it. I'm not joking about the hobby bit; I still haven't decided what to do when I grow up. After having ditched the absurd idea of becoming a scientist, I didn't know what to do in life, so I decided to buy some time doing things that interested me. I studied music theory, started a choir and entered into acting, directing and writing for the student theatre, along with arranging music for the orchestras and bands performing in them. Having taught the violin for a year, I played the drums in a band for a short while. I didn't know how to play the drums, but it was a punk band, so I suppose this was an asset. Our band played one gig before we split. Eventually I ended up at a proper professional theatre as an assistant director and producer, and it was here that someone spotted an advert in the papers about the film school and suggested that I should apply to it.

Looking back at all of this, my choice of career makes sense. There is a clear pattern, even if I didn't see it at the time. So, what did I learn from life and the things I did before becoming a director?

I learned that the conductor decides on the repertoire but is not the one making the music. The singers and musicians do. The conductor only guides them.

I learned that when you stage a play, it's not you the audience comes to watch. They come to see the play, the actors, the decor and to have an experience. If the play is a success, credit goes to the ensemble. If it's a flop, the blame will fall on you.

When I made my graduation film (where I brought in many of the crazy friends I had worked with for years but who had never made a film before), I learned that it was them bringing in horses and steam engines, designing pyrotechnics and shipping in whole school classes as extras, etcetera that ultimately made the film come true. Not me. I just asked them for help; I knew who and how to ask. I was the keeper of the idea, and by exciting them in the way that I told them the story, I made them want to be part of it and to perform a string of miracles. So here's my definition of what a director is:

The director is the Keeper of the Idea and the Protector of the Film.

My graduation film went on to win a whole string of international awards and is still running in festivals and cinemas all over the world. Every time I watch it again, I think of my friends who made it possible. It's a humbling thought that without them there would have been nothing on the screen.

*

I have worked with a lot of people since in my career. Producers, actors, runners, grips, cinematographers, boom operators, designers, art directors, scripties, gaffers, sparks, 1st, 2nd and 3rd ADs, sound recorders, editors, assistant cameramen and women, pilots, production managers, line producers, track layers, production assistants, executives, stand by props, mixers, publicists, carpenters, painters, Steadicam operators, drivers, stuntmen, crane operators, extras, armorers, animal handlers, helicopter pilots and security personnel.

An overwhelming majority of them were really nice people. Why? Because they were good at their job and had nothing to prove beyond that. Difficult people are often hiding their insecurities by being unpleasant and divisive.

SO:

If your idea of a director is someone who swaggers around the set looking cool in a leather bomber jacket, boots and sunglasses, with a viewfinder around the neck, calling everybody darling, or shouting at people when they haven't brought the bits of Mars bars cut up in the 2.3 centimetre bits they asked for two minutes ago, or frequently using phrases like 'Don't worry, I know what I am doing' or 'Do you know who I am?!' — think again. Do yourself and the rest of us a favour: grow up or pick another job. There are too many of that kind around already.

But if your idea of a director is someone who is an enabler, the one with the ideas that will inspire others to do amazing things they have never done before, who is there to fight for The Film and not their ego and who understands that The Film is King, then you stand a good chance of becoming a good — even great — director. And you will have a lot of fun.

This is the essence of this book. I won't tell you *how* to make a film but *how to think* when you're making one. I hope you will find it useful!

Chapter 1 - A GUN FOR HIRE

Let's say you are a director who's been offered the chance to direct a script written by someone else. What do you do? Well… you read the script and then decide if you want to direct it or not. Sounds pretty simple and straightforward, and it is when you've been directing for a while and have worked with other people's material before, but it is not when you first set out and I will explain why.

First of all, if you're a relatively inexperienced director (having made less that three films) and someone asks you to direct a film based on someone else's script, you will be so flattered that your first action (after you have hung up and danced around the room, punching the air like a footballer) will be to ask your friends out to buy them a drink and celebrate that 'you've arrived'. The next day, you will wake up with a hangover but with a grin on your face as you to start working on your award ceremony speech before deciding on how to spend your fee on things you always wanted and desperately needed, like a string of new outfits, a new laptop and a state of the art video camera.

In other words, you have already said yes before you have read the script and chances are that you will, even if you hate it.

That's what I did.

Perhaps it doesn't matter too much if you love or hate a script when you are desperate to direct a film (as you will find further down). If your ambition is to make whatever is in front of you now the best thing you ever made, then go for it! But to do that you need to find the right angle and have a clear idea of how to achieve this. That idea will come to you when you read the script for the first time.

Chapter 2 - HOW TO READ A SCRIPT

The first time you read a script for the first time is the last time you read it for the first time.

You only read a script for the first time once.

A script only gets one chance of making a first impression.

Why did I say that three times? Because it is very important! In my experience, it's during the first reading, and the short time afterwards, that you actually make the film, even if you're not aware of it yet. This is when your instincts start feeding your subconscious with stuff to process into the big idea you will bring to the film (some people call it the vision). The second time you read it, you already know what is going to happen, so the element of surprise is gone, and with it, your instinctive ideas. So here's my advice:

GET RID OF THE CAT

1 Find a quiet room with a comfortable chair. Turn off your phone, computer, radio and TV to eliminate anything that will distract you. If you have a cat, put it out in the garden and lock the cat flap. Then, pretending you are in the cinema, read the script from beginning to end in one go as if you were watching a film.

2 Next, put the script away and run a hot bath or go for a run or do anything else that prevents you from taking notes. Me? I will opt for the bath.

3 When the bath is ready, drop yourself into the hot water and re-live your first reading. Play the movie as you remember it back and forth in your mind. All the things you really liked, whatever stood out and the things you didn't understand will pop up to the surface — but don't get out of the bath tub to take notes. Not just yet! There is no rush, the water is still nice and warm. Stay where you are until you're desperate to get out, and then stay a little bit longer.

4 Get out of the bath and make notes. If you had any good ideas while soaking away in the bath, you will not forget them. If you had a bad idea, hopefully you will. Write down all your thoughts without stopping to read them back, edit them or to put them in any kind of order until you've finished writing. That comes later!

Make notes of:
1 What you liked about the characters and why.
2 When and if they made you laugh or cry, or in some way touched you.
3 Any fun, exciting or scary moments.
4 Any other scenes or moments you liked (even if they didn't work).
5 If there were any scenes or sequences that would make a good set piece.

A set piece is a sort of 'film in the film', usually one or many scenes in a sequence that forms a freestanding entity; in an action movie, a car chase would be one set piece and a fight scene another. But a set piece can also be a short, but very important moment in any story you want the audience to pay extra attention to: I once turned a very short scene where a doctor is waiting in his car for a moment before stepping out and walking up to a house into a set piece. It was central to the story, and it's now on my showreel.

Try to avoid thinking about the things you didn't like or things that didn't work. They will always be there (because no script is perfect), but it's the good stuff that will guide you on how to fix what is not so good, so always focus on this.

6 Next, put your notes away, make yourself a cup of tea and go to bed.

ZZZZZZ

7 When you wake up the next day, your mind will have worked while you were asleep (every psychologist in the world will tell me this is nonsens), but the point is you slept on it. If you had any more thoughts, write them down straight away.
8 Now you can read the script a second time and make more notes.
9 When you're done, organise your notes and add to them. As you do this, your intuition will locate that grain of sand around which your idea will eventually form and take shape like a shimmering pearl. It usually takes a day or so, sometimes more, but you must allow your mind to play with your ideas before you start locking them down and come up with solutions (unless they are very obvious!).

This is a period of grace. It's a time filled with magical discoveries and lightbulb moments. It's the memory of these that you will feed on up to the moment the film is finished (if you decide to make it), because from here on it will be just hard work.

Chapter 3 - THE IDEA

Before I became a director, I studied chemistry at university. A writer friend once asked me if there were any similarities between this subject and what I was doing now, and if I had learned anything in chemistry that I could make use of when making films. I thought about this for a few days and came up with this:

LET'S PLAY SCIENCE

In chemistry, when you want to work out what a molecule of liquid X looks like, you're facing a tricky task. Molecules are very, very small (even the big ones). They are so small that you can't see them. Not even with a microscope. Even if you could build one that was extremely strong, you would still have to shine so much light on the molecule to see it that it would start behaving differently from how it normally behaves, so you still wouldn't know the answer.

There is a way, though, and it is based on our understanding of how molecules work. If you take a larger amount of liquid X and freeze it, then it will turn into a solid object called a crystal. The clever thing about this is that inside the crystal, all the molecules will line up next to each other in a perfectly regular pattern. Think of the audience on one side of a football stadium. They sit in straight lines looking in the same direction. That's what the molecules in a crystal do too.

Next you put your crystal on top of a pin. On the wall behind it, you put up a big photographic plate and opposite this you place a strong light (like a laser). When you fire the light at the crystal, it will behave like a prism and break the light. If you've seen the sun shine on a chandelier, you will how noticed that the sunlight will break into different coloured dots in all shapes and sizes in all the colours of the rainbow. This happens here too, and this is why we put the photographic plate behind the crystal before we switch the light on. The plate will catch whatever pattern the light splits into, and when you develop that plate, you will see a pattern of dots where the light hit it.

By measuring the position, size and intensity of all those dots, you can work out, backwards, what the molecule that formed the crystal must look like to create the pattern you see. It will always look different depending on what molecule you used to make the crystal.

SO WHAT DOES THIS HAVE TO DO WITH FILM?

Think about it. An idea is just like a molecule — something you can't look at and can't see.

When you shine a light on the crystal, it creates a pattern on a screen. Looking at this pattern, you can work out what the molecule looks like.

When you show a film based on an idea, you project a pattern of actions and events on a screen. When the audience watches the film in the cinema, it looks at this pattern of actions and they can work out, backwards, who the characters really are and what the story is about.

Same thing.

SHORT SCIENTIFIC CONCLUSION

An idea is a thing that doesn't exist outside your own brain. But if you turn it into a physical object (a film), you can project this on a screen. If you get all the elements right, if they are all carefully selected and perfectly lined up to support the idea, then the idea will become real in other people's minds, too, and will stay with them.

Here's a picture of an idea magnified 1,000,000,000 times (it's that red spot in the middle):

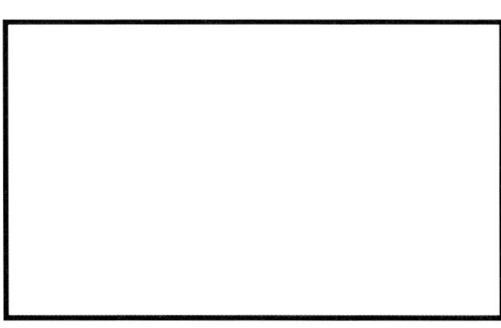

Chapter 4 - IS THAT A YES OR A NO?

Did you have an idea and do you still want to make this film? Before you can answer this question, there are three more factors to consider. The first one is time. Can you fit the film into your schedule? Let's assume you can. The second is money. There is only a small group of directors that do not need the money, so let's assume you do. The third is the producer.

You've read the script and have an opinion about it and a meeting booked with the producer to pitch your ideas. You will soon find out what he or she thinks of you, but it's a good idea for you to look at the producer first to find out what YOU should be looking for. (The same rule applies when you're trying to find someone to produce a script you wrote yourself.)

REMEMBER THIS:

'Filmmaking must never be a mechanical process.
It's when a group of people
who have learned to trust each other
come together to perform miracles.'

Chapter 5 - THE PRODUCER

If you ask someone who doesn't work in the film industry what a producer is, they will tell you that he or she is a person who raises the money so that you as the director can go off and make your film. Allowing for some obvious exceptions, this couldn't be further away from the truth of what a producer is — or should be, if they're any good.

Let's dispel some myths:

1 People calling themselves producers are not always producers. They could be people who never made a film in their whole life calling themselves producers because that's what they want to be.

2 Being able to raise money doesn't make anyone a producer. It makes them a fund raiser.

3 There is no such thing as a 'creative producer'. All good producers are highly creative.

4 A producer is not someone you can 'add later' to sort things out.

A good producer is a person who recognises a good idea when they see one and can judge its potential on its own merit, and who understands what makes it good and what it will take to make it good and can communicate this. If they are willing, ready and able to do this, they will not settle for anything else.

When you are about to make a film, the producer should be with you from the start. You must be able to think of him or her as your professional partner. Your companion. Your fellow traveller. Someone you share your artistic vision with and who sings from the same hymn sheet. Someone you can bounce ideas with, laugh and cry with and someone who will give you their full support if things go wrong. The joint creator and the other parent of your baby, also known as The Film. Someone who has an equal interest in the project from the beginning to the end and beyond.

In short, the producer should be your best friend. Never settle for anything less.

MUTUAL TRUST AND RESPECT

The best way of finding out if you're meant for each other is to sit down and talk about the idea and the script until you're blue in the face, until you have turned every stone over and there is nothing left to talk about. You dissected it, you agreed on it and you came up with the comedy version of it that made you both laugh. You will have a shared vision, and this will make the film a better film. And if all your instincts then tell you that you are a perfect match, chances are that you are.

If there is a niggling doubt that you decide to ignore, or if your eager brain says yes but your instincts tell you no, and you still decide to go ahead with this person and it all ends in tears, I promise not to say 'I told you so.'

But I did 'told you so'.

Chapter 6 - POSSIBLE OUTCOME

So, let's say you made your best pitch ever: the producer loved you and offered you the job. How will your meeting with the producer help you to make your decision?

There is no clear cut answer to this, but I will give you some possible scenarios. I use the word producer here in a broader sense, it could also stand for a commissioner.

1   If you love the script and get along with the producer like a house on fire, the answer is, of course, yes. Chances are this will be your masterpiece.

2   If you love the script but the producer has a very different idea about what the film is, think twice before saying yes. If you're passionate about it, then it's up to you to prove you're right. If you can, well done. If you can't, then you're in for a bumpy ride where someone will get hurt — and that somebody will be you. You will probably learn a lot from the experience, but it will cost you and you will only know years later if it was worth it.

3   If the script is just okay but you get along with the producer, chances are it will be a fun project to do. You will both spur each other on to find ways of making it great.

4   If the script is just okay and you don't get on well with the producer, say no.

5   If the script is crap but the producer is really supportive, then you have nothing to lose. Make it, take the money and run. Remember, you don't have to show it to anyone.

6   If the script is rubbish and you hate the producer, forget it. Believe me when I tell you that no one needs money that badly.

So, let's assume you liked the script, found that the producer really IS you best friend and you said yes, signed a contract and pre-production starts on Monday. What's next?

A FOOTNOTE:

How do you find a producer if they didn't find you:

1 If you've been to film school, chances are that you have already met this person.

2 If you have friends that you are as close to as the Cohen Brothers are, you do what they did. Work together and make films.

3 Watch films and television dramas. If you see something you really like, make a note of the producer's name, then write them a letter telling them you really liked what you saw and ask if you can buy them a cup of coffee to talk about it.

Chapter 7 - PRE-PRODUCTION

Pre-production. Or prep. Whatever you call it, it's the period of time when you work through every single detail of everything you and the crew are going to do until you have finished the film. If you do it well, there will be no surprises during the shoot. If you fail, you will be gambling with the success of your film.

Pre-production is when you make the film.

The famous film director Alfred Hitchcock used to hate the shoot. It bored him stiff. He had already completed the film in his head, and now this his clear image of it would be sullied by the process of turning it into a physical object. If you can see the finished film the way he could, then you have prepped yourself well. And you will understand that it will never be exactly like that. It will be better — or worse.

In chapter 1 I made a statement:

> 'The director is the Keeper of the Idea and the Protector of the Film'.

Let me try to explain what I mean by telling you about a guy who lived around 400 BC and whose name was Plato.

Plato was a great philosopher who spent most of his time walking around and just thinking about things. He was rich and didn't have to work for his living, so he could afford to this.

One of the things he thought about was reality and how we experience everything around us. How do we, for example, define something as obvious a chair? Think about it. There are thousands of different chair designs. You might say that a chair is something with four legs you can sit on. Ok, but what about the chairs that have three legs, or two or just one? Some have back rests, some don't. Some have arm rests, and other's don't. If you were to come round to my place for dinner and I asked you to bring an extra chair, you might come with a box or a stool and they would still qualify as chairs because you can sit on them. But the fact that we can sit on something isn't enough to make it a chair. You can sit on a rock or a tree trunk but we wouldn't call them chairs. Clearly there is, somewhere, an idea of what makes something a chair even if we can't define it.

So if we can't define it, how come we still know it's a chair?

Plato explained this by saying there are two worlds:

1   The Ideal World
2   The Real World

The Ideal World is where the idea of a chair can be found (and other things that us mere mortals know what they are but can't define because we can't see the idea of a chair).

The Real World is the place where we real people live. Plato describes this as a cave where we all sit with our backs to the opening, from which the light flows in, hitting the cave wall in front of us.

When the ideal version of a chair is waved in the light behind us, we will see a shadow of it on the wall in front of us, and we will recognise it as a chair, even if we can't look straight at it (this is pretty cinematic... Maybe Plato invented the cinema without realising it).

What happened when you, the director, had your great idea, is that you went to the Ideal World and came back. You have seen what the idea of your film is. At every point through pre-production, when someone suggests an object or a solution to a problem, you can, and will, compare it to what you saw in the Ideal World.

As the protector of The Film, you will know which shadow on the wall to pick. You have seen the light. For the rest of the prep and shoot, it's up to you to answer questions by describing what you saw in there the best way you can and making the right choices.

That's all.

And if you don't know the answer, just say so. Then listen carefully to what people in your crew suggest because chances are they know. If they are experienced, they've been to the Ideal World long before you and they all know how to make a film.

IMAGE TIME

You've seen an image of the idea. Here's an image of the director building a line of defence around it to protect the idea:

And here's a picture of the producer building a second line of defence around the entire production:

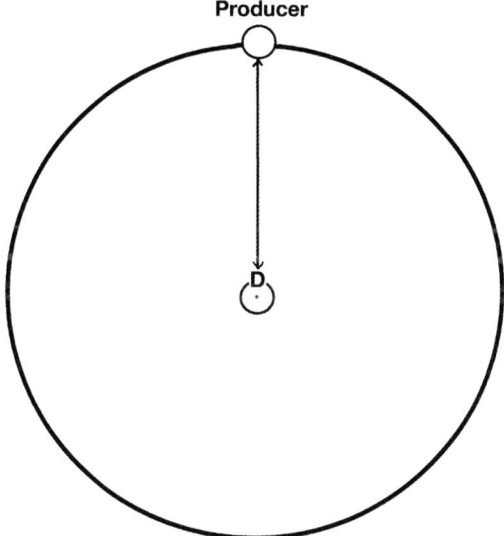

Let's go find the people who will help the two of you make it all happen.

Chapter 8 - CREWING UP

On your first day at work you will start working on a lot of things: You will be doing your notes on the script, you will be looking at the first version of the schedule and, parallel to this, you will start picking the crew. A film crew is structured into a number of departments.

> Assistant Director Department
> Art Department
> Location Department
> Camera Department
> Sound Department
> Continuity
> Costume Department
> Make-up Department
> Post-production
> Production Department

When you crew up you select the heads of department: a designer, a first assistant director, a location manager, a director of photography, a script supervisor, a sound recordist, a costume designer, a make-up artist and an editor. Depending on your project you might add visual effects and a stunt coordinator to the list. The Production Department is usually already in place.

These are the people you will work with throughout the production, and they are the people who will produce the material that will make the film. Each department (with one exception) will be joined by a number of other crew members that often come along with the head of department and will not be picked by you (with a few exceptions).

A designer, for example, often brings his or her own art director along, the director of photography brings his or her camera team and the sound recordist has his or her preferred boom operator. This is great because they are up-and-running teams-within-the team with a built-in element of trust.

THE DREAM TEAM

There is a lot of fantastic talent out there. If there is someone you know or have worked with before – or someone you would love to work with — then you and your producer will discuss them all and make a list of your first choices (the 'dream team').

In this process, you will first find out who is available. Good people are usually busy. Still, a person who is busy one week can be free the next because projects get delayed, postponed or cancelled.

As the list of people you like fills up, you get in touch with them or their agents.

SELLING THE FUR BEFORE YOU SHOOT THE BEAR

The next step is to interview them. I will talk about interviews in more detail in the chapter about casting, so I suggest you read that before the time comes, but the long and short of it is this:

Every interview is a two-way thing. It's not just you picking them, it's them picking you (on behalf of themselves and their co-workers). They might have a few other projects in the pipeline that they won't tell you about unless they become an annoying obstacle or a good excuse to say no.

First, you introduce yourselves and make small talk about things you have worked on before, what you like and what you think of the latest movie you both watched, etcetera. This is a good way of finding common ground; if the other person hates everything you like, then pay attention to how they react during the next step. If they need the job rather that want it, they might tell you the things you want to hear rather than the things they will do when you start shooting, and by then it is too late).

YOUR PITCH

After the small talk, it's time for you and your producer to make your pitch. You should practice this (or at least decide who says what) because you must speak as one, with the same passion about the project to make it clear that your big idea and your vision is shared. If you put your heart into it and think of each person you interview as the most important team member in your crew, you will find that you get better and better at making your pitch. If you can excite them the way you are excited, make them laugh and cry the way you did and make them see the film as you see it, they will all be prepared to drop everything to follow you just because they want to be a part of your project. They will want to work with you. You will have the luxury of choice, and the dream team will be yours to work with.

YOUR FELLOW TRAVELLERS

Let's start with the people who are usually already there when you arrive — the Art Department. (When you see the letters HoD after a title, it means that they are the head of department.

Chapter 9 - THE ART DEPARTMENT

PRODUCTION DESIGNER (HoD)

The production designer (or just designer) is the person responsible for the overall look of your film and everything you see in it. This is one of the first people you should get on board when you set out to make a film (if your producer hasn't picked them already).

Good designers are highly sophisticated people with the rare ability to combine abstract theory with a direct and practical approach; they know a lot about everything from architecture and construction, how to burn a house down without burning it down and other special effects, to how to cheat things and how to support stunts. They can enrich your understanding of your own film with references from various periods and from art history, and they can make good use of colour theory.

In short, a designer is a pragmatic dreamer. He or she will express and translate the abstract ideas of the film into planks of wood and paint. They will enhance already existing locations by adding things, replacing them or often by just taking stuff away. Or if the place doesn't exist and you have the money, they will build it — either in in a studio or on a location. If you're good at explaining the idea, they will make your film better if you let them.

During prep, every time I feel tired or get stuck on how to do something, I always drop in on the Art Department because they are fun, inventive, creative, curious and inspirational people who love their job and a good challenge. I have, if only platonically, fallen in love with virtually every designer I have worked with and I still count many of them as good friends.

ART DIRECTOR

If the designer is the pragmatic dreamer, the art director is the person taking responsibility for the technical side by translating the ideas into plans and drawings. This is another very close working relationship, where the art director is the designer's right-hand person. Experienced art director often move on to become designers.

PROPS BUYER

This is short for property buyer, and this is the person who sources objects and other stuff you need your actors to handle in the film. We're talking anything from vases to put flowers in, the flowers that goes into those vases, the pocket watch grandpa is checking in the opening scene, the gun the hero is slinging in the final climax, to the villain's get-away car.

The prop buyer will go through the script with a fine toothed comb and list every single object that appears there. Then, at the earliest possible date, they will sit down with you and ask you a million questions so you can explain and describe exactly what it is you want these objects to be, do and look like.

From then on, you will be bombarded with samples and suggestions for you to approve or not. This is an ongoing process throughout the entire prep period and, if you explained yourself well and the prop person is good, they will find you stuff that is way better than you yourself could ever have thought of, and this alone will make your film a better film.

More often than not, props are rented from props houses (the cost is usually 10% of their value) and cars from specialised car hire companies. If you need something that doesn't exist (like a space knife made out of glass with a built-in blue light), the prop buyer will probably make it for you.

Why? Because just like the designer and the art director they are your best friend.

THERE'S MORE...

If you're working on a big production, there will be a whole string of people working in the Art Department, most of whom you will not deal with directly. Some of them you will only catch a glance of when you arrive on location in the morning (thinking you are the first person to arrive) just in time to see them leaving, having put the final touches on the set. They are the stand-by carpenters, stand-by painters, construction people, etcetera, but I won't explain what they do because I guess you have already figured it out. There is one stand-by person you will meet on a daily basis and that's the stand-by props person.

STAND-BY PROPS

Stand-by props is the person organising and handling all the props you use on set. This can be the same person as the props buyer, but it doesn't have to be. If they're good and well organised (an absolute must!), they are worth their weight in gold. It is a stressful job so treat them well and show them your appreciation whenever you can.

Props are very important, not least for the actors. Often they depend on them! If a prop is missing or not right, chances are that it's your own fault because you didn't check it before the shoot. If your prop person has forgotten to bring a prop or even lost one, they will feel ten times worse about it than you do. So, instead of wasting time and energy on getting angry, do your job and find a solution to the problem while they are looking for a way to replace the missing prop. If Francis Coppola could continue shooting *Apocalypse Now* when his lead actor Martin Sheen was in hospital for three months after having suffered a heart attack, then you can find a way of shooting around a missing birthday cake until a replacement arrives (I know this because it happened to me). If it happens over and again, then it's probably a good idea to replace this person or shift the responsibility to somebody else.

You now have two new best friends:

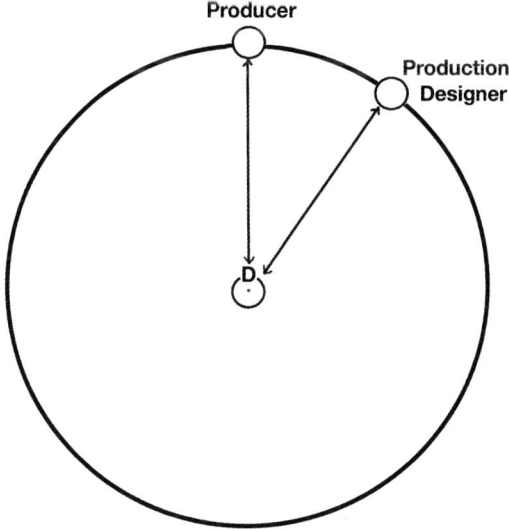

Chapter 10 - ASSISTANT DIRECTORS

FIRST ASSISTANT DIRECTOR (HoD)

The first assistant director (1st AD or the first) is neither an assistant nor a director. The 1st AD is the head of a department made up by the 1st AD and the 2nd AD, plus one or more 3rd AD's. They all do distinctive jobs and operate at the very heart of a film shoot. The best way to describe it is that when the filming starts, they are the masters of the universe and they run the show (not you) because they are in charge of the almighty schedule.

THE SCHEDULE

During pre-production, the 1st AD is responsible for creating the shooting schedule. I say creating, because scheduling a film is an art form that takes as much skill and talent as directing and producing.

The schedule is the master plan for how you are going to organise the shoot and in what order the scenes and shots will be filmed. If your film takes place in a single room with a single actor and the story evolves in real time and is done in a single shot, then you probably don't need one. You just all turn up in the morning and work until it's done. For anything more complicated than that, you do, because there are always a number of reasons why one order is better than another.

Think of all the variables you will have to deal with: actors' availability, location availability, travel time, make-up time, costume changes and, not least, the weather — to name but a few. They will all constantly change and so will the schedule. The schedule is never done; it's a living thing and arguably one of the most powerful tools you have to help you achieve your ambition and realise your dreams.

The 1st AD will help you make it so, so you should choose them well. Working on the same script, a not-so-good scheduler will probably sink your film. A good scheduler will make it possible, and a great scheduler will not only make the impossible possible but will allow you to finish on time without any unplanned overtime. I've experienced them all. So:

The 1st AD is, without a single doubt, your best friend.

SECOND ASSISTANT DIRECTOR

The second assistant director (2nd AD) works very closely with the 1st AD. He or she is never on set but is based in the production office or at the location base if you're on location. The 1st AD and 2nd AD are usually in contact with each other via radio or walkie talkie.

So, what do they do? You could say they are the human face of the production, because they meet and greet the actors when they arrive and make sure they know where to go to get changed into costume and when they are expected in make-up.

In the office, they prepare the call sheet for each day. They co-ordinate transport and the pick up of actors to and from the set and keep a log of the progress on set. They update the schedule and the callsheet (let's say you don't complete all the scenes on day one and decide to pick them up the next day) and hand it out or email an updated version to the cast and crew before heading home.

THIRD ASSISTANT DIRECTOR

The third assistant director (3rd AD) is the highly qualified 'runner' and the 1st AD's right-hand person. If you have extras in a scene, the 3rd AD looks after and organises them, and if the 1st AD has to leave the set, the 3rd AD steps up and becomes 1st AD until he or she is back.

Mr TERRY

I've worked with a 1st AD called Terry a couple of times now. He is a good friend who finds time to work with me between productions like *James Bond*, *Tomb Raiders* and *The Mummy*. He will always remain one of my favourite human beings because he is in possession of a crystal ball. This extraordinary man's scheduling skills are so accurate that he once predicted a 20 minute over-run on day three, week two, of a BBC drama series we were making together. Come that Wednesday, twelve minutes into the over-run, an agitated producer appeared on set demanding an explanation as to why we were doing unauthorised overtime. Terry calmly explained that he had anticipated this and had left all the necessary information on the producer's desk three weeks earlier. The producer denied this, told Terry he couldn't possibly have known this and gave him a piece of his mind before storming back to his office to take a look. He didn't return. The information was, of course, on his desk. We finished 21 minutes late that day, the extra minute caused by the producer's interruption.

Your three new best friends:

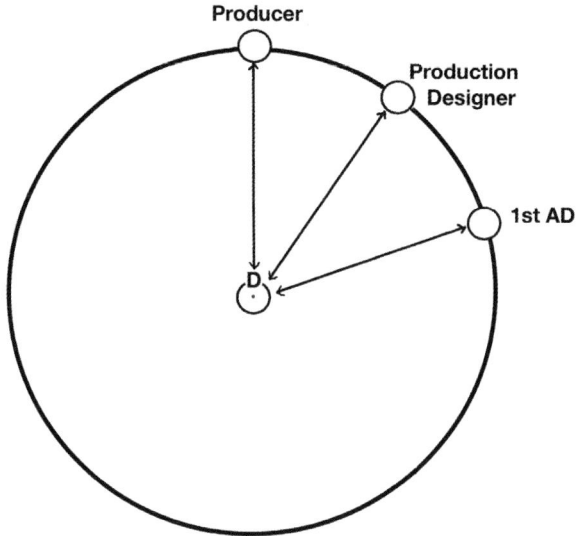

Chapter 11 - LOCATION, LOCATION, LOCATION

The person who finds a location for you is called the location scout or location manager, and this is someone you should get on board as soon as possible! Believe me when I tell you that during pre-production and the shoot this person is your best friend.

With the perfect location, your scene will be better in more ways that you can imagine. It will not just end up looking great on screen, but the location will tell you how to shoot the scene. Without the location, you will not have a scene. At all.

So who is a location manager? In short, it's a person with local knowledge of the area in which you are going to film, who also knows what makes a place suitable for film production.

STEP ONE

After you have hired your location manager, it is important to spend time with them going through the script in great detail. They need to know:

1. What character a place belongs to and what you want it to look like.
2. What you want it to express in story terms.
3. Any specific technical qualities the location needs to have.

Let's say you are filming in North Yorkshire and you are looking for a remote cottage. There will only be so many remote cottages in that area.

If it is important that you can look from the bedroom straight into the kitchen through the hallway, that will narrow down your choices. If you are planning to do a lot of tracks in the kitchen, you will need a cottage with a big kitchen. And if you are looking for a cottage with a big kitchen plus a straight road leading up to it (because your whole vision for the film is based on a particular way of staging the last scene using this straight road), then the number of choices are probably down to one.

If you use a really good location manager, he or she will probably know this cottage already, or at least know where to look for it. If they are very experienced, they will probably suggest one or two places, visit them straight after the meeting and show you pictures or a video the next day.

If you use someone who isn't a location manager, you will probably end up waiting a week for the same result. Even if they find it, that week they spent driving up and down country roads is wasted for you because you can't work on your schedule or plan your shots before you have your location.

So, if you want to save time and money and want peace of mind, hire a professional!

STEP TWO

After a while, your location manager will take you on a trip to show you the places they have found that meet your brief. This is called a recce (short for reconnaissance, pronounced 'rekki'). Your designer should come with you because they are able to see a place for what it *can* be rather than for what it is. If they are busy with other things and you end up finding a place you really like, your designer can come along next time because you will go back at least once.

What I'm going to say now is really important:

The location you imagined when you read the script doesn't exist. Trust me, it doesn't. The places you will see will either be better or worse — but they will never be as good.

When you go to see a location for the first time, expect to fall in love with it. Think of it as meeting a partner-to-be that's been picked for you without you having a say in the matter.

Just like a partner for life, a location is everything for you as a filmmaker. Never reject a place at first sight; look at it as if this is the only location in the world and work out how you would shoot it if you had to do it there. It will put your ideas to the test and teach you something new about the scene. If your designer isn't there, you still won't know what it's going to look like after they have waved their magic want around. So, if it's not completely and totally wrong, keep it in mind. At least until you see the next one.

Remember that even if you find your perfect location, you might lose it. If, meanwhile, you work out how to use a place that is second best, you will have a back-up plan and won't have to start from scratch if this happens.

I have, on more than one occasion, shot a scene in a location that was plain 'wrong' but have ended up with something far more interesting than I expected.

STEP THREE

Let's say you found what you think is the perfect location. You might think the job is done, but it is not. Your location manager's work has only just begun.

Here's a list of the things he or she needs to do now:
1 Negotiate a contract for the hire of the location (can the production afford it?)
2 Secure a site close to the location for the unit base.
3 Work out the logistics of parking, electricity, holding areas, toilets, security, etc.
4 Secure permits from the local council and talk to the local police.
5 Find out if there are local events like football tournaments or kite flying festivals taking place on the day you are filming.
6 Inform the local community about your plans for filming there.
7 Make maps and record and write driving instructions on how to get there from multiple places.

Any of the points 1-5 can rob you of your choice.

STEP FOUR

Go back to your location as often as you can, or at least once after finding it. You will draw inspiration and get ideas when spending time there, and you can check that your shot plans will really work.

Even if you don't find the time to return during prep, you will go there at least once more before you start filming, and that's at the technical recce (see Chapter 31)

ASSUMPTION IS THE MOTHER OF ALL DISASTERS

Remember that finding the perfect location is only the beginning. Further down the road during prep you might lose it (people owning property often change their minds) or the schedule might tell you that your favourite location is so far away from the other locations that it doesn't make sense to travel there.

This is why you should remember the places you didn't jump at when you first saw them, because they might end up saving your life.

FOOD FOR THOUGHT

Finding a location is often far more difficult than you think, even if what you are looking for seems simple and straight forward. While working as a mentor at the Met Film School in London, I remember a very good script set in a terraced house with one important scene taking place in the basement. The film had to be shot near the school, which is located in a part of London called Ealing, where there are around 23,000 terraced houses. No problems there then... The student location manager (who didn't know London very well) worked very hard. He went up and down the streets dropping letters in hundreds of letter boxes asking if they were interested in letting us use their house as a location for two days for a small fee, but he got no replies at all.

Throughout the two week pre-production, the team had daily production meetings ticking off things that had been achieved. Each day, the location manager told them 'no location yet'. You could see how the energy of the group started to fade. The production was in limbo. More people went out dropping letters in letter boxes and knocking on doors, but still, nothing. With only three days to go, morale was so low that the crew was ready to give up on the whole film. Two days before the shoot, the production manager found a house without a basement and someone volunteered to build a basement in one of the classrooms and it all worked out well in the end.

But why could they not find a location?

For the simple reason that houses in Ealing don't have basements! A professional location manager would have known this, but that's not the point of the story. The point is the lessons they learned:

1 Never assume that something will be easy.
2 Never wait around for something to come to you.
3 Always have a back-up plan.

In short, assumption is the mother of all disasters.

Still, the 'leaflet in the letterbox' does work from time to time, so use it as one of your methods to find a location if you can't afford a professional location manager.

And remember: when you ask to film in someone's house or on their land, there is, strictly speaking, nothing in it for them. Think about it... Would you give up your home for a day or more just because a stranger wants to make a film? Not unless you were offered something in return. Money usually helps, so if you have a budget, then that puts you in a good position. But money is not enough, you have to make them excited about the project and make them want to be part of it. Being polite and charming is a good start. Telling the story in an exciting way helps too. And if a well-known actor or actress is going to be in one of the scenes filmed in the house that usually clinches the deal. But sometimes even that isn't enough.

MARY

I worked with a fantastic location manager a few years ago. Let's call her Mary (because that's her name). Mary is very good at psychology. When we were out on an early morning location recce a few years ago, I saw this big house at the end of a road that instantly ticked every box in my mind. I knew I wanted it; I needed it and I had to have it, and I told Mary so. Recognising the expression on my face, she pulled up in front of the house, smiled and said 'Wait here.'

Stepping out of the car, she walked up to the house and rang the bell. There was no one at home, so she knocked on the house next door and spoke to the people there and then she crossed the road and spoke to the people in the two houses opposite before returning to the car and me.

'So?' I asked her. She told me that the people living in the house I liked were very precious about their home; they were away on holiday but would be back tomorrow. 'Let's go back tomorrow then?' I suggested. 'No', said Mary, 'let's go back the day after tomorrow.' 'Why?', I asked. 'You'll see', she replied.

So we went back two days later at 11 o'clock. Instead of going to my house of choice, Mary first checked the other three neighbours' houses (taking her time, knowing they would have gone to work) before walking up to the house I wanted and ringing the bell. The door was opened almost immediately by a middle aged, rather posh woman. Mary greeted her with a big smile, showed the lady an ID before introducing herself and me, explaining who we were and that we were looking for a film location.

But instead of asking the lady if we could look at her house, Mary started asking her about the neighbours, who they were, what their houses looked like inside and when they would be back home. It only took a minute before the lady invited us inside to take a look at her house, and another three for her to suggest that we should use her house and not any of the neighbours'. A quick look around confirmed my instincts — it was the perfect location — so we shook hands and she signed a release form.

Back in the car I asked Mary 'How did you do that?' 'Well', she said, 'the neighbours told me about the lady of the house and her husband, and I soon worked out that they are not only precious about their house but about their status in the street. Leaving it for a day meant they would hear about the film shoot from the grapevine and that we were looking for a location [word usually goes around quickly about film shoots]. If we filmed in one of the neighbours houses, they would be the talking point for the next year or so, and so I figured that the lady of the house wouldn't want to be sidelined (why have you looked at their houses and not ours?) and played on her vanity.'

It was a bit of a gamble but it paid off. Mary's gambles usually do because she understands how people think and knows how to ask. Needless to say, she is still a very good friend of mine.

FINALLY

If you are planning to shoot a film abroad but can't afford to travel back and forth to find your locations, find a production company operating in the area where you want to shoot and make them co-producers. Chances are they will know people who have enough local knowledge to find what you are looking for and, if they love your idea, will find extra funding for the project.

If you are a young filmmaker who wants to make your own short film, my top advice is to first think of a location you know you can get, then write a film set in that location.

Your four best friends:

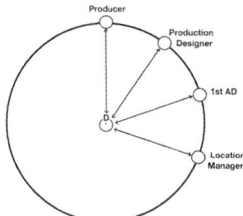

Chapter 12 - THE SCRIPT SUPERVISOR

Also known as continuity or scripty. The scripty is the head of a one person department. It is a highly sophisticated job that demands good organisational skills, a very good memory and an acute sense for details. During the shoot, the scripty will save you from making small or big mistakes at least ten times a day. You probably know the long and short of it already — length of cigarettes; in which hand they held it; when a line was said, etc.

But way before then, during prep, the scripty will give you something that will affect each and every decision you will make.

TIMING THE SCRIPT

The first thing your scripty will do when joining the production is to time the script. This is done by reading it with a stop watch in hand, making a note about each scene and then adding up the whole. Again, this is an art form that takes practice. Two experienced scripties have been known to time the same script and, when comparing results, find that they are just one second off. After a conversation with you about how you will shoot the film, they will go off and time it again, and make adjustments based on what you told them.

WHY IS THIS IMPORTANT?

If the film is for television, the length of a film or programme is already fixed to plus/minus a few seconds. The sooner you find out that your script is too long or — God forbid — too short, the better, because it gives you a chance to do something about it. When you start shooting, it's too late. You can't stand on a location and make big decisions about what to cut or what to add; that's what your prep-time is there for. Plus, if you end up shooting 70 minutes of material for a 60 minute programme, you will have spent time working on things you won't use instead of spending that time on the stuff you will keep.

So your scripty will have saved you before you have even started filming.

PROTECTING THE FILM

Next, when you start shooting, you will already know roughly how long a scene should be, so you will know if a scene is stretching or speeding up. If a scene plays out longer than expected, but is fantastically brilliant, you can start thinking about how to accommodate that. If you notice that every other scene plays out a bit too short (filmmaking is never a mechanical process — the actors might speak faster than you anticipated) you will have to find extra material or else you will be in deep trouble. Believe me when I tell you that there is nothing worse than having to stretch a film in post-production. Even the most wonderful material will be robbed of its pace and rhytm, and that always turns a potentially good film into a bad film.

Finally, if you make many takes in a long dialogue scene and things start to sag because actors are getting tired, chances are the material will not cut together particularly well because the various takes will have a different pace. Your scripty (who is timing every take) will point this out to you when it happens, so always keep them close.

AN ADDED BONUS

When I shoot a comedy scene, I always keep an eye on my scripty. Why? Well, he or she is the person concentrating hard on a million things going on on the screen. If they laugh, the comedy has penetrated all their defences and the moment must be fun!

In short: you now have five best friends (which is even better than four).

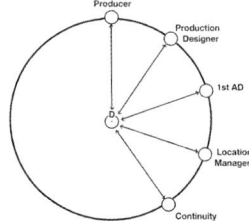

Chapter 13 - CASTING

Finding the right actor for every single part in the script is crucial to the success of your film. If you don't, you will have compromised yourself before you have even started shooting. So how do you go about finding them?

THE CASTING DIRECTOR

If you have a budget, using a casting director is money well spent; brief them well and they will have the knowledge and the instinct to help them find the actors you are looking for. They will know who is available and who will be prepared to be in your film. They also have a working relationship with actors' agents, which will dramatically increase your chances of casting someone well known, if that is what you are looking for. They will also know of up-and-coming talent and have intimate information about things you won't find on a website or in CVs etcetera.

FIND THEM YOURSELF

Go to the theatre, go to the movies and watch TV. Make notes on actors you like and collect them in your own database.

Going to see plays in the theatre is something you should do regularly, even if you are using a casting director or plan to use internet facilities. Not West End plays (they are very expensive and you probably know the actors in them from other things you've seen already) but plays in pubs, fringe theatres, graduation shows and actors' showcases. These are inexpensive and sometimes even gratis.

If you see an actor you really like and who could be perfect for a part in your film, just walk up to them afterwards, tell them you loved their performance and offer to buy them a drink. You don't have to tell them about your film straight away, but if the following chat confirms your instincts, ask them if they would be interested in coming for an interview.

THE INTERNET

Casting Call Pro and Spotlight (to name but a few) are internet search facilities. The basic principle is this: you create a new project for your film, upload a synopsis and descriptions of the actors you are looking to cast. Whoever is out there reading this will write you to say they are interested. All you have to do is to sift through the replies, decide who you are interested in meeting and then contact them.

*

Whichever route you choose, you will end up doing one or more casting sessions where you meet a string of actors to interview them for the various parts in your script.

If you work with a casting director, they will take care of all the practical arrangements – all you have to do is to turn up on the day.

If you do it yourself, you will need to organise a suitable location, communicate with the actors and organise a schedule, send out script pages with notes on the characters and print hard copies of the scene to be used at the reading, along with preparing everything else you need on the day. This is a time consuming process, so don't leave it too late during your prep. The sooner the better.

On the day, you will need an assistant to look after the actors while they're waiting for their turn to show them the way from the waiting area to the room where the interview is taking place, take messages about delays, and supply refreshments. If you already have a crew, ask your 2nd AD or a production assistant to do the job.

Think of casting as an evening out when you are hoping to pick up a partner – for the evening or for life. You spot a person at the other end of the room and you find yourself drawn to them. This is always instant. If you're brave, you make your way over and you strike up a conversation. During this conversation, you will either get closer to this person or not. You will tick each other's boxes or not. If you do, you know you have found someone who is the answer to all your dreams.

Casting is just that. Nothing more, nothing less.

THE CASTING INTERVIEW

There is a simple protocol for how to perform a casting interview, and there's a reason for this which I will explain later in this chapter. You might read this and think that this is not exactly 'rocket science…'. Still, this is how you do it, and if you do it right, you will do it well. You'll be surprised by how many directors there are out there who are not particularly good at it. I know this because hundreds of actors have told me so.

1 THANKS FOR COMING IN

When the actor enters the room, you stand up, greet them with a welcoming smile, shake their hand and introduce yourself. If there are other people in the room, it's your job to introduce them too. (If you work with a casting director they will do this)

Invite the actor to sit down and ask if they would like something to drink. Actors usually say 'no thanks' because they want to save you the trouble, or they don't want to waste valuable time. If it looks like they've run all the way, give them some water anyway.

2 RELAX

If the actor seems nervous, the best thing is always to ask them straight out if they are nervous. If they say 'yes', tell them that so are you, 'but there's no need for you to be, we're all friends here'. If they say 'no' — tread carefully. They are either very insecure, lying or just very, very sure of themselves.

3 LET'S GET TO KNOW EACH OTHER

Spend two or three minutes making small talk to break the ice. Talk about the weather, how long the journey in was, if it was good or not and if the place you're casting in was easy to find. If the actor had a nightmare journey or had problems finding the place, you want to know this before you move on.

Keep the conversation light and general. Remember, the sole purpose of this is to keep them at ease, relaxed and comfortable, so you can get a clear idea of who they are. Ask them what their favourite part or project has been to date, the one they enjoyed the most. This will make them talk about something they love, and they will do so with a passion from which you will learn a lot about what makes them tick.

This is important:

Never, never, ever ask an actor what they are working on at the moment!

First of all, there are a lot of very talented actors out there, but the competition is fierce so the odds of them not having worked for a while and with nothing in the pipeline are overwhelming!

Imagine how you would feel? It would make you insecure, tense and probably defensive as you go through the nos and the rejections that are still gnawing at the back of your mind.

Secondly, you want them to like you. Casting is a two-way thing. While you are trying to figure out if they are right for the part (if you don't already know this from the way they walked in), they are trying to figure you out and whether they want to work with you: whether you're clear and concise, if you know your stuff, if you're honest and if you understand the directing process.

Most actors are, by nature, very generous when 'judging' a director. If they've come to see you, it's because they want the part. If they get it, they will make sure they do it well — with or without you. What they are hoping to find is a director they can trust, for whom they are prepared to throw themselves artistically, because they feel you will be there to catch them if they fall. In short, if they get a sense that you know what you're doing, they will give you a great performance because you make them feel safe.

4 DO YOU MIND READING?
When the small talk is over, always ask if the actor would be happy to do a reading. They will say yes, but it's polite to ask.

If you haven't sent them the scene beforehand, or if they haven't had a chance to read the text before they arrived, give them a couple of minutes (or as long as they need — within reason) to familiarise themselves with it. If you have sent it, offer them a chance to have a quick look at the text again to refresh their memory.

5 ANY QUESTIONS?
Ask the actor if the scene is clear and if it make sense to them, or if they have any questions about the story or the character. If they do, give them short, clear and concise answers. Never give a full length rendition of the story or plot, just stick to what they need to know (who they are and what they want) to understand the moment and the scene they are going to read. If your answer is more than 30 seconds long, chances are that you haven't done your homework properly. If your answer is 60 seconds or more then you're in trouble — you probably don't know what the scene is about yourself.

6 LET'S READ
Before I go on to the reading, remember that the director never reads opposite an actor in a casting interview. Someone else does. The director's job is to look and learn.

7 THE FIRST READING

The first reading: if the first reading is perfect, great. The script is good, you've explained your intention well and the actor has done a great job. Uncork the champagne and discuss what you're going to wear at the premiere screening. No, seriously... if the first reading was perfect, do it again! But this time change something. Tell your actor they love the other character instead of hating them, or anything else. It will demonstrate to you how good the actor is at taking direction.

If the first reading didn't go so well, quickly work out why, if you don't already know it. Perhaps you didn't explain yourself well enough. Fine-tune the description of the scene and the character's thought process and do it again.

8 THE SECOND READING

If you changed something after the first reading, you may learn something new about the scene, or how it can be played in a way you hadn't thought of. Even if it's not what you want for the film, it will make you see the character from a new and fresh angle that could open a door to a deeper understanding of your story.

9 A THIRD READING?

If you have time for it and you really like the actor, have fun with it! If you already know that the actor is not a contender, don't.

Remember: you don't do the reading to get the final performance; you do it to get to know the actor and get a sense of who they are and what they can do.

10 THANK YOU!

Always say: 'That was great, thank you very much!' and compliment the actor on their work. Even if they are wrong for the part, they have still spent time preparing themselves, they have travelled across town or further and possibly taken time off work/organised a baby sitter/ rearranged their day, to come and see you at their own expense. In short, you owe them.

11 BEFORE THEY LEAVE

Stand up, shake their hand and say: 'Thank you very much for coming in.' Ask them if they have any further questions. If they do, answer them briefly. Tell them if you are planning on seeing more actors for the same part and inform them when they can expect to hear from you if they have got the part or not.

And here comes a really important bit:

12 THE DATE

Give them a date when they will find out if they got the part or not. Even if you haven't decided yet on that date, you must let them know this.

Why? You have just given someone hope. From the moment an actor leaves the interview, their 'waiting game' begins. Finding out if they got the part (or not) is crucial. They could be putting another job on hold for you. Perhaps the fee you're paying them (big or small) will save their home and marriage. You don't know this, but by interviewing an actor, you have given them hope; it could represent a turning point in their career. It's an important promise to keep.

FOOD FOR THOUGHT

Socrates, when getting dressed in the morning, always put on his toga first, then his right sandal and then his left. He never deviated from this. Every morning, same routine.
This allowed him to spend his time getting dressed pondering philosophical matters rather than wasting time making mundane, every-day decisions.

If you keep the casting ritual simple, it leaves you with the freedom to concentrate on why you are there: to get to know and form an opinion of the person in front of you. To do this, you need to switch off your intellect and only listen to what your instincts tells you.

TRUST YOUR INSTINCTS

If you know your character inside out, chances are you will know if an actor is right the moment he or she steps through the door. If you don't, or if you're not certain, you will have another 14 minutes and 59 seconds to find out. If they are, you will.

During the fifteen minutes you spend with each actor, all you are doing is waiting for the moment when you can see this actor being the part and you see the movie with them in it, and it gives you a buzz.

If you still don't know for sure, or if you are uncertain, then he or she is probably not right. You must still pay attention because they might be the closest thing you will meet.

And finally: on a number of occasions, I have cast an actor in a different role than the one they'd come in to read for. If you don't sense the right vibes from the outset, try seeing them in another part and use the second and third reading to imagine them as that other character. If there is something that chimes, don't hesitate: ask them if they want to read for this part too, give them this set of pages and ask them to come back half an hour later, or when there's a gap in your schedule. I have never had an actor say no, because it doubles their chances of getting a job.

THE RECALL

A recall is when you ask an actor to come in a second time. Perhaps you think they are right but you're not one hundred percent sure. Or perhaps you have two or more candidates that are all good but in different ways, so you need to work out which of the differences will serve your character best.

Actors like being recalled. It means they are in with a good chance, so they will be prepared to throw themselves at it now that there's more at stake. If they crumble under that pressure, this in itself will inform you about your choice. In short, you will get to know them much, much better.

If the first interview is fifteen minutes long, the recall should be half an hour or more. You let them read different scenes and spend time discussing the part in more detail. Based on this, you then go away and think about it again before you make your decision together with your producer.

If you're still not sure, you call them in a third time.

ROMEO AND JULIET

Next, you might need to test the lead actors' together before you can make your choice. Let's say, for the point of argument, that you are going to film a version of Romeo and Juliet. It's not enough to find the perfect Romeo and then the perfect Juliet; you need to know if there is chemistry between them, if they click.

Why is this important? Well... go back to the beginning of the book where I talked about the idea and think about it. The story about Romeo and Juliet is not about him or her at all. It's the story about the magical connection between them. Two 'star-crossed lovers', the instant love that out-ranks every other love, the thing between them you can't see. If that is not there between the actors, then there's nothing.

So, you make a shortlist of, say, two or more contenders, recall them and try them in all possible combinations. You may well find that the third choices on your list are the ones that really hit it off and generate the emotional magic you are looking for. If it still doesn't happen, start casting all over again.

A trick is to ask the actors if there is someone they would like to work with, someone they really 'fancy'. This could be someone you or your casting agent hadn't thought of or didn't know about. If not, you're still a bit wiser because you have a better understanding of what it is that makes this particular actor so attractive to them, and this can narrow down your options.

I used Romeo and Juliet as an example here because the point of the story is so clear. The element of chemistry between actors is applicable to virtually every film. There are usually two characters at the emotional heart of a story. Make a list of movies you've seen and you will see that I'm right.

THE REST

When you have decided on your central characters, the rest is usually a straightforward business. You're creating a cast around the leading actors that will support the way you want them to be perceived.

THE WRONG WAY AROUND

When the director Milos Forman (*Amadeus*, *One Flew Over the Cuckoo's Nest*) cast his actors, he recalled them over and over again before he gave anyone a part. When he made his film *Amadeus*, he found an actor called Tom Hulce and soon decided on him playing the part of Mozart. (If you haven't seen this film, do it now. It's one of the great masterpieces of modern time and it won 10 Oscars). Milos knew that the moment he gave an actor a part, they would relax because they were already destined to become stars. So, by recalling them over and over again, he kept them hungry and willing to listen so he could rehearse them up to the point when he thought they were ready. THEN he gave them the part.

FOOD FOR THOUGHT

I learned everything I know about casting by making one single serious mistake. Today, 20 years later, I still wake up in the middle of the night thinking 'why didn't I cast actor X?'. The story is simple. I was going to make a film in Scotland and we met virtually every actor available. On day three, actor X stepped in through the door. It was 'love at first sight', and we instantly got on like a house on fire. The interview and reading were perfect. We went out for drinks afterwards and there was an obvious connection between him, me and the part he was up for. So why didn't I cast him? Because — and this is painful — I thought he *looked* wrong.

I'm going to repeat that last sentence, just to rub it in: I thought he looked wrong.

I wasn't listening to my instincts. Looks have nothing to do with it. Looks are not character or personality. They are just — looks. It's who the actor is and what he or she projects that is important and what count. Nothing else.

Since making this painful mistake, I have cast around 400 actors and I'm proud to say I've only made one semi-mistake since. That's pretty good considering, and it is all down to that single mistake. When you cast looking for an actor to play a character, looks are pretty far down the list. It's who they are, and what emotions and sensualities they project that counts. Full stop.

Your six best friends:

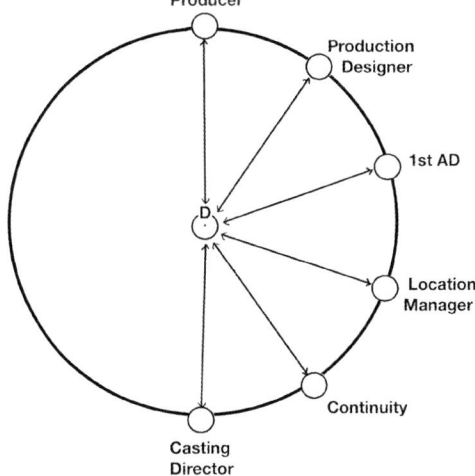

Chapter 14 - CAMERA DEPARTMENT

DIRECTOR OF PHOTOGRAPHY (HoD)

The director of photography — or DoP — is also known as the cinematographer, lighting cameraman or just cameraman. For the simple reason of gender neutrality I will use the term DoP because it makes most sense. Lighting camerawoman sounds a bit... odd.

The DoP is responsible for lighting the film and is in charge of the camera crew. To do this, he or she will need a lot of help, and this is why the Camera Department is usually the biggest department on a shoot. DoPs often have a regular team working with them (camera assistants, etcetera) so they will bring them along. You can read more about who they are further down.

The sooner the DoP arrives at the production the better. At times they will only join you on a full-time basis halfway through the prep period. This is not unusual and I wouldn't worry too much about it. Good DoPs are often very busy. And, thinking about it, you will have been too. Sorting out the script, getting the other departments up and running and casting is hard and time-consuming work. So by the time you sit down to talk about visuals, you will have relaxed a little, with the added bonus of being better informed and prepared for what you want to do.

Remember that the DoP will have had time to think about your project ever since you explained your vision at the interview. And there is nothing stopping you from talking on the phone or emailing pictures and references, even if they are working on something else.

THE PLOT THICKENS

First you update the DoP on the progress you have made so far. You go through changes in the script and you look at any actors you may have cast and the locations you have secured.

Then it's time to talk again about the overall feel of the film and agree on 'the look'. You do this from a character and story point of view. Take your time; it's important that you agree on this before going into any detail. (Don't forget that this will change and evolve as you go along.)

You will discuss what you want the camera to do — lots of hand-held shots, tracks or static shots, etc. (Don't forget that this will change and evolve as you go along.)

ACTION

The sooner you go to look at locations and the studio (if you are using one) the better. The designer should come along too.

It is important to look at the studio even if the sets are not built yet. The shape of the room in combination with the designer's explanation of the lay-out is a very important starting point for the DoP's lighting plans. If much of the filming is studio-based, this will affect the way he or she will light the locations when you film there so it will match.

When you recce the location, you will show and explain the way you want to stage the action so the DoP can work out the best way to light it. Be prepared to make changes to your plans. Again, the layout of the location will determine if what you want to do is possible to shoot. You will also work out when the best time of day is to shoot various scenes, depending on where the sun will be at a certain time of the day.

Straight after the recce, the two of you will sit down with the 1st AD to go through everything you discussed on your recce so he or she can accommodate this in the schedule and work out if it is possible to do or if you have to modify or re-think your plans.

By the time the DoP comes on, the schedule will take over the role as king.

A quiet word of caution here, which may or may not apply to your production, but it is something I've experienced on more than a couple of occasions. DoPs' tend to think they are the most important person in the crew. This is of course true, but so is everybody else. Always remember that.

OPERATOR

The camera operator is the person who operates the camera. Nothing else. Sometimes the DoPs operates the camera themselves, giving them full control of the image. The advantage of using an operator is that it allows the DoP to concentrate on just lighting the set.

Whoever is doing the job, this is the person you will have an extremely close working relationship with. You will decide on the shots, but if they are good they will add to, and enrich, every frame and make your shots better than you could ever imagine because it's the only thing they have to do. Keep them close!

FIRST CAMERA ASSISTANT

Or the 1AC, also known as the focus puller. Now... I know I said this before, but this person, if they are good at it, IS your best friend. Being a great focus puller means you are the person with one of the most highly rated skills on any film set. Let's assume the light is going and you have another 60 seconds to get a 50 second shot in; it will all be for nothing unless the focus puller gets it right so the first take stays sharp all the way through. A great 1AC will do just that. And when they do, they will have saved your film. If they do it over and over again, you owe them. Focus pulling is a talent. A rare one. You can either do it or not. Just like the guy who shuffles coal on a steam train is the person who actually drives the engine, the focus puller is the person who will catch the performance and get you the shots — or not.

SECOND CAMERA ASSISTANT

Or the 2AC. He or she does everything around the camera that the 1AC doesn't do, like moving the tripod, swapping lenses and shifting the scripty's monitor around. Although this is a very physical job, most 2AC's I have worked with have done it with a smile on their faces because they can't wait to be upgraded to 1AC and then move on to become a DoP. Look after them and make sure they keep that smile on their faces by appreciating their work!

GAFFER

In short, the gaffer (an old English word for 'boss') is the chief electrician and the DoP's right hand when it comes to lighting a set. A good gaffer usually knows a lot about lighting and, if they're good, will anticipate what the DoP wants and will always be a step ahead.

SPARK

A spark is an assistant electrician working for the gaffer. They are the guys who will rig the lights, run the cables to plug them in and then stand outside in the rain propping them up if the light is shining in through a window while a storm is raging outside. Then he or she will wipe themselves and the equipment dry and pack it all away while you pour your first glass of wine after the day's work. If they, or any other member of your crew, turn up in the same bar as you, buy them a drink. They all deserve it.

GRIPS

Here's another position where you can find people who are virtuosi at their work. The grip is responsible for handling the camera hardware. They will be rigging the tripod, laying tracks, operating the dolly and fixing the camera to cars, tracking vehicles, crane and jibs and making sure it is all safe.

Just as the focus puller is crucial to the successful execution of a shot, so is the grip. Try to find out who they are and their level of skill while you are still doing your prep. It will affect the way you think about how you will shoot your film.

ASSUMPTION, TRUST AND INSTINCTS

While making an episode of the BBC drama series *Hamish Macbeth,* we were staging a singing competition between two rival villages. The singers were to perform standing on a big boulder in the middle of a beautiful valley where the ground was pretty rough. To heighten the experience, I wanted the camera to make a wide shot in a 90 foot semi-circular track and suggested using a Steadicam for this, which the producer agreed to.

The grip on the production was a man named Joe. This extraordinary man and his crew knocked me sideways on day one of the shoot when they laid an 18 foot track from a field across a ditch into a road in under 20 minutes (they finished before the camera department had even set up the camera)! Having told me on the tech recce that he could lay the 90 foot track for me in under an hour, I decided, for some reason, to stick with the Steadicam for the shot. Asking me why, I told him I was worried about time — the Steadicam was fast and that the ground was too soft. He just shrugged, looked at me and smiled.

Que Mr Steadicam... He was good, but the ground was, well, soft, and walking sideways while keeping the shot perfectly level when his feet keep sinking into the ground was very difficult. Two hours of trying later (with an additional three hours spent in post production to compensate for the wobbling camera), we almost got the shot I wanted, but only just. I should have listened to Joe. I should have done what Stanley Kubrick did on *Full Metal Jacket* and trusted his expertise... He knew this would happen and he told me so, but I had already made up my mind and didn't listen.

Your seven best friends:

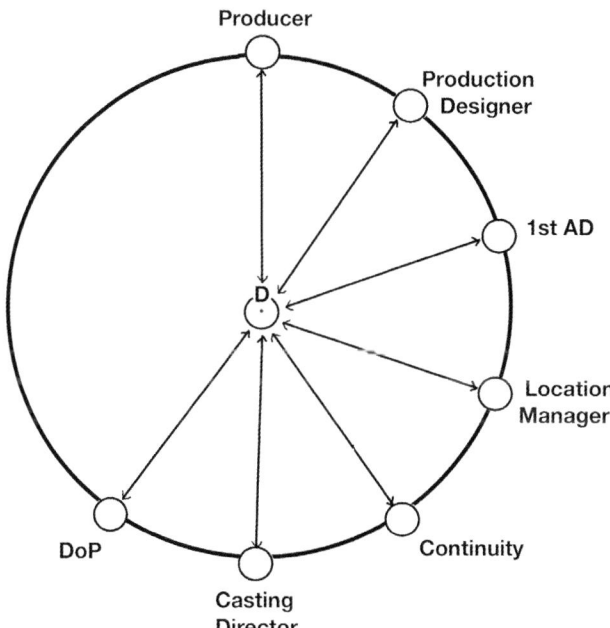

Chapter 15 - SOUND DEPARTMENT

The historical difference between television and a film projected in a cinema is that TV added pictures to sound (radio) and the movies added sound to the pictures. Silent movies that used to get away with telling the story in pictures have now developed into an art form heavily dependent on sound, sound effects and music.

In a film, sound has a number of roles to play. First of all, you need to hear what the characters are saying when they are speaking. Secondly, when they don't speak, the sounds they make when walking, sleeping or just sitting still will make them real and three dimensional. Thirdly, the ambiance (or the silence of a location) will shape the viewers emotional response to a scene. Complete silence is no longer an option.

What I described above are the sounds you record during the shoot. The sounds you add later, during the edit and the process of track laying (that's where a sound editor creates and adds sound effects), will help the audience to focus on what is important in a shot and draw attention to this.

But:

Nothing will never, ever beat, replace or compensate for well-recorded sync sound. However clever your sound effects people are in post-production and however good the actors are at post-synching dialogue, it will always end up being second best. This is why your friends in the sound department are the most important people on your film set.

THE SOUND RECORDIST (HoD)

The sound recordist is responsible for the recording of the sound when you are shooting your film. Seated by the recording device (usually organised on a trolley that can be moved around a set or location with great ease), he or she will direct the boom operator by communicating through a local intercom system which is part of the sound recordist's equipment. (This is one of the reasons they always wear headphones. The second, and most important, reason is that it allows them to hear what th,ey are actually recording.)

BOOM OPERATOR

The boom operator is the person who sticks the microphone into the space where it will best record the dialogue or any other sound generated by the actors.

*

Most people think the sound recordist (SR) is the most important person, but in my experience this is not strictly true. The boom operator and the sound recordist are equally important. I have worked with some extraordinary boom operators and found that the quality of the sound was fundamentally down to his or her skills in getting the mic into the right position. One or two of them managed to catch sound that was so good that when mixing the final soundtrack it could be used as was!

Having said that, the sound recordist's experience will enable the boom operator. Further to this, when you use radio mics or multiple microphones, nothing can ever replace the skill, experience and technical knowledge of a good SR. They will also know how to eliminate noise generated by your own equipment (a very common problem).

So, why do I speak at length about how the Sound Department works on set when this is a book about preparations? The answer is — anticipation.

By the time you hit the set, camera will always take precedent over sound, and you will often be seduced into sacrificing the sound for a good shot. Think about how a film shoot works. You watch the actors performing, you decide on the shot, you put down the camera and then everybody else has to work around it. When the lighting is done and you want to know why you can't start shooting straight away someone will tell you: we're waiting for sound. This will make you believe that sound is slowing you down. They're not. They are just quietly trying to negotiate a way through an obstacle course of lights and shadows created by the camera department. A good DoP will make this easy for the boom operator, a not so experienced DoP won't always know how to.

In the heat of the moment, you will be made to believe that the sound can be fixed in post-production. Here's your wake-up call: it can't. If you don't get it on the day, you won't have it. It's as simple as that. And if you don't have it you are, well, screwed. Don't wait until you are sitting in the cutting room to find this out. Prepare for it.

FOREWARNED IS FOREARMED

The Sound Department is usually the last to join the production because there's not much for them to do in prep. What you can do, however, is to go through the script with them and explain exactly how you plan to shoot every scene. The sound recordist will understand 'the nature of the beast' and devise a strategy to resolve any upcoming problems. If you are going to use a lot of hand-held cameras or will be shooting dialogue scenes from a distance in big locations where it will be impossible for the boom operator to get close enough, you can plan in advance when to use radio mics. Radio mics are not magic; they are a compromise because the quality is never as good as that of a boomed mic. If you know when to use them, they will work in the bigger scheme of things.

Radio mics also take time to rig, but if you know you are going to use them and have prepared for this, then the 1st AD will allow time for it in the schedule and you won't lose any valuable shooting time.

WILD TRACKS

Wild tracks are called wild tracks because they are sounds recorded separately and not in sync with a picture. Typically, the sound recordist and you will have worked out a list of important sounds you will need in the finished film that they will collect during the shoot (door slams, running water, bells tolling, etcetera). But — they are also a useful method of getting around problems when recording dialogue.

When you've finished shooting a scene, you stand all the actors around the microphone and have them play out the scene again. They will still be in the 'zone' of the performance they've just given, so the pace, rhythm and inflection of the words will be consistent with what you have just filmed.

This is something you should plan for, allow time for and build into your schedule and your daily work routine, to make sure it gets done. When in post-production, you'll be surprised how often you can just to drop the wild track of the dialogue into the film and find that it is in perfect sync.

Assumption is the mother of all disasters, so do them even if you think the sound recording in the scene was good. It will also allow you to vary the performance a bit, and this usually comes in handy in the edit.

And then they were eight!

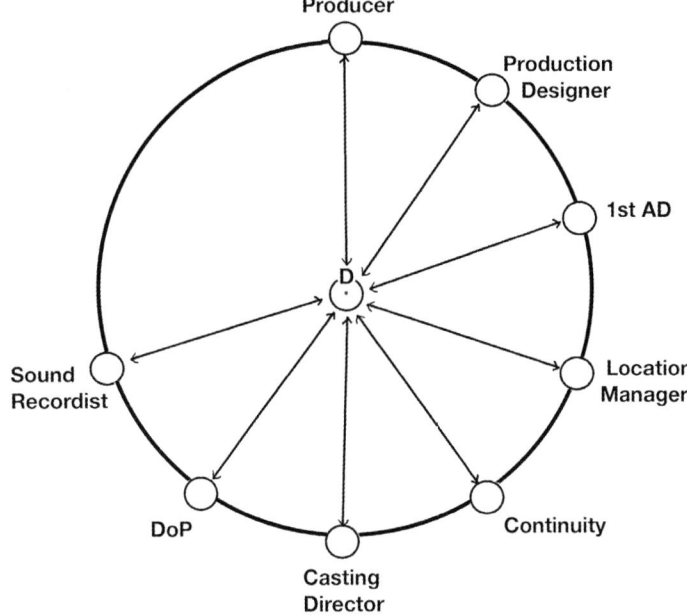

Chapter 16 - COSTUME DEPARTMENT

COSTUME DESIGNER (HoD)

An early, preliminary meeting with the costume designer is another thing you should add to your list of priorities. I say preliminary because before you have cast the actors, you won't know what is going to work. Costume is all about narrowing down the options, so you will spend a lot of time talking about the characters, who they are and what you want them to project.

The next time you meet, the production designer will be there and you will discuss the colour scheme. (unless you've already done that.) You may have decided to de-select a colour. Look carefully next time you see a movie — red, green or yellow can be missing from the palette. Or be very dominant.

Based on this, they will do a lot of research and come up with ideas, often presented with mood boards and drawings. This is an ongoing process where you will like or dislike things as you go along. Again, it's about narrowing down your choices.

When the actors have finally been cast, the real work begins. The costume designer will organise a session where each actor will try on an abundance of clothes. You will normally not have time to sit in on this, so the costume designer will take lots of photographs for you to look at and to make notes on. Sometimes all the suggested costumes work, sometimes none of them do. Sometimes the entire character can be defined by a single coat, shirt or hat, even if you didn't plan for them to wear any of those. Costume designers are highly creative people with very open minds who can translate your story and the psychological development of a character into clothes. In short, let them loose and they will expand your own understanding of what you are about to make. If you trust them and your instincts, they will make your film a better film.

Sometimes an actor hates what you want to dress them in, and if this happens, the negotiating skills of the CD, and their ability to re-think their ideas will be put to the test. It's important that the actor feels great in what they will wear. If they don't, they will hate every moment of the shoot — because you insisted on them walking around looking like an idiot and they won't trust a single thing you say to them.

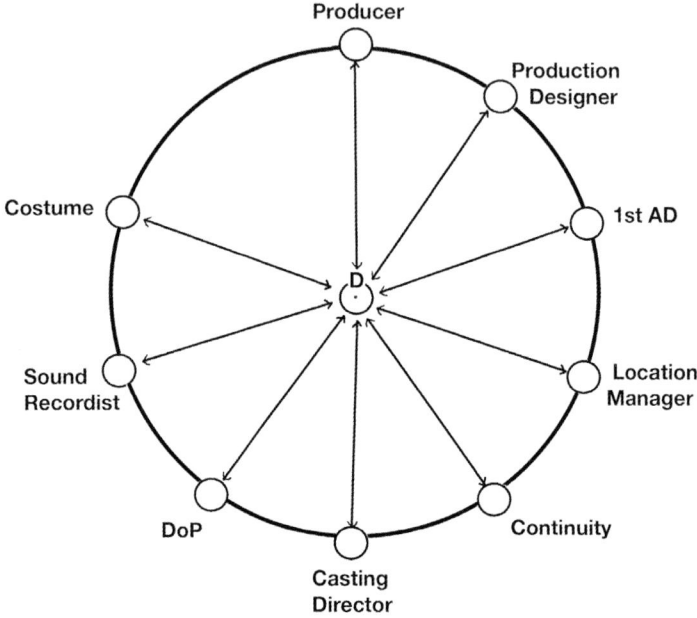

Chapter 17 - MAKE-UP DEPARTMENT

Your work with make-up is very similar to your work with costume. If I copied the content of the previous chapter into this and replaced the word costume with make-up it would more or less make sense because their workflow during prep is the same.

You sit down together at the earliest possible stage and go through the script in fine detail and discuss every aspect of the characters and the story. Armed with this understanding, they will go off and do their own research to present you with material that will explain what you can play with to enhance and underpin a character's mind by manipulating their hair and the surface of their skin. Again, this is a fine art where less is more. If it is done well, the strange side effect is that it will be perfectly invisible to the audience.

INVISIBLE?

Yes.

SO WHAT'S THE POINT...?

That IS the point. If you notice the make-up, there's usually something wrong with it. The most important part of the make-up artist's job is to make sure the actors' looks are consistent between various camera angles throughout a day, a week, a month. If you still find this confusing, here's what you should do:

STOP THE CLOCKS

When you wake up tomorrow morning, take a selfie when you're brushing your teeth after breakfast. Then take a pic of yourself at lunchtime, followed by one at the end of the day. Repeat this over two weeks or a month (if you're going to shoot a feature film).

Put the pictures on a timeline and flick through them. Notice how your face and hair constantly change?

This is what make-up deals with. A shot you did in the morning of day 1 might have to cut straight to a shot you did in the evening of day 25. In story time that's 1/25 of a second. In real life 25 days will have passed. Still, the face in the two images has to match. If it doesn't, the truth of the moment is gone. If it does, no-one will ever notice. That's what make-up does. They take care of continuity. They are magicians. Treat them as such, and they will make your film a better film.

OMG

Make-up has a secondary, very important yet informal part to play. That of the psychologist/therapist/priest. When an actor arrives on set, the first thing they do is to go into make-up. Make-up time = confession time. Sitting in a comfortable chair first thing in the morning, the actor will vent their joys and frustrations about life, love, work and everything else that has happened since the last day of shooting. They make conversation the way you you do when you have your hair cut. The make-up artist listens to it all and will end up knowing more about the actor's private and professional life than perhaps they want to.

Again, for you as the director, this is a rich source of information to tap into. If you create a good working relationship during prep (where you learn to trust each other), make-up will keep you up-to-date on how your actors feel, and if there is something traumatic going on in their life that may affect their work with you on set. There is nothing sinister about this. More than often, an actor will share information knowing — or hoping — it will be passed on to you so they don't have to make excuses that will interfere with the creative process in front of the camera. Forewarned is forearmed. Any information shared must always be treated as confidential and can never be referred to, but it will help you in your work.

Your ten best friends (not counting the other 20 something best friends I listed in the various departments.) And there's still more to come...

NO PYRAMID?

By now you will have worked out that the structure of a film team is not a pyramid (as most people tend to think, with the director at the top.) It's not. It's a wheel; a wheel where the idea is the nave, the crew makes up the tyre and the spokes created by the constant flow and exchange of ideas.

We've come back to the producer and the people working for him or her. In short, we've come full circle.

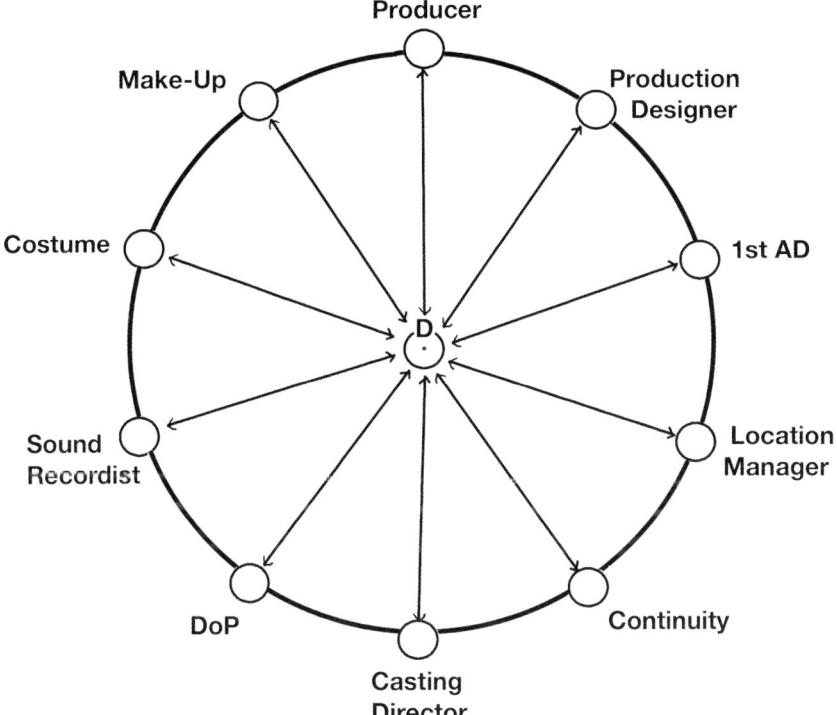

Chapter 18 - PRODUCTION OFFICE

The production office is the powerhouse of the production; the engine that keeps everything and everybody moving forward. There's a strict (but flexible) hierarchy at work here, with a lot of talented people with an impressive set of skills — the most important being the ability to multi-task. The Producer is HoD, and here are the people working for him or her:

LINE PRODUCER

If you and the producer are the two parents of the film, the line producer (LP) is the house keeper who oversees everything from the budget (with the producer), the schedule (with the 1st AD), and the contracts with all the actors and the crew. Being the flexible best friend of both you and the producer, the LP has a very exciting and hands-on job handling the inevitable clashes between schedule, budget and your ambition to find a way of saying yes. In short, he or she is a highly creative enabler. Keep them close and they will do everything within their power to find a way of making all your dreams come true.

The line producer will join the crew from the start of the prep and stay on a for a week or so after you wrap the shoot. He or she will, in other words, not be involved in the post-production

PRODUCTION MANAGER

The production manager (PM) works directly under the line producer. When the LP and you have worked out what you want to do, the PM will micro-manage the budget and schedule to work out all the details. Say, for example, your film or television programme has a very big set piece to be shot at night; chances are you will need some extra sparks on that day. The PM will work out how many you need and how many you can afford, and will find them and book them. He or she will also deal with invoices and other boring stuff.

PRODUCTION CO-ORDINATOR

The production co-ordinator (PC) works directly for the PM. Their job in the office is very similar to what the 2nd AD does on the set. In short, they co-ordinate (the name is a bit of a giveaway). This is a support function to the LP and PM, producing all the paperwork and booking everything from cars and other transport you need to hotel rooms for the actors.

PRODUCTION RUNNER

The production runner is the office equivalent of the 3rd AD. They run, print, drive, pick things up, drop them off and do everything else the PC asks them to do. If they're good, they may well be a PM, a PC, an LC or a producer in the future, so be nice to them too.

TIP OF THE DAY

The production office is always busy, and there is always someone there. Make sure to show them your appreciation, because without them you are nothing. Tip: everybody likes to get a bunch of flowers from time to time. If you keep the bunches coming your new best friends in the office, they'll look at them every time they are working late (which they often do, sometimes very late), knowing that you are thinking of them.

Chapter 19 - POST-PRODUCTION

POST PRODUCTION CO-ORDINATOR

In the 'old days' — when people shot films on film — there weren't that many PPCs around. The editor and the assistant editors could handle most things themselves (almost). Since the world of filmmaking has become more or less digital, this has become a very, very important job.

With an endless number of standards and formats around, any film production today has to create a strategy in the early parts of prep, to define and create the specific workflow that will best serve and support the film you are about to make. In the 'old days' when shooting on 16 or 35 mm film, the DoP could pick the camera model they personally preferred or the one that 'sat best on their shoulder'. Whatever camera make they picked, the end result would still come out on the same strip of film that would eventually be cut and then spliced together again in the lab. Those days are gone.

The technical development of equipment moves so fast now that what is true today is not necessarily true tomorrow. Look what happened when the RED camera first came out. It changed everything. Then the Alexa came and re-wrote the standard again. A producer friend of mine use to say that we still live in a 'digital stone-age'. I think he's right: there's much more to come and every production needs someone who knows everything about it.

The PPC will work very closely with the camera and sound department throughout the production, from beginning of prep until the film is completed.

DIT

Here's another relatively new and important job: the digital imaging technician (DIT). If you are working on a big project, the DIT will be part of the camera crew where they collaborate with the DoP on how to best set up the camera for what he or she wants to achieve and keep this consistent.

If it is a small production, they will do another job, too, that of the data wrangler. The DW collects all the image and sound material on a daily — sometime hourly — basis, making sure everything is ok while transferring the information from cards to hard drives, then backing this up again on multiple hard drives. Video technology is very versatile, but the scope for something going wrong at any step of a production is enormous. One faulty card and a day's work is lost. In the old days of film, your images actually existed — you could pick up a roll of film and look at them. Today it's just code and lots of it. Knowing you are working with a good DIT will make you sleep better at night. When you start shooting, make sure to keep yourself informed about the wellbeing of your material by checking in with the DIT and your editor on a regular basis.

THE EDITOR

I will not talk about the editing process itself in any detail because this is a book about how to prepare. But it is important to understand what editing is. I said earlier that the ability to raise money doesn't make a person a producer. I'd like to add to this that ownership of a computer with editing software doesn't make a person an editor. A major film school in the UK teaches editing under two separate headlines: 'editing' and 'creative editing'. The interpretation of the word 'editing' here is how to operate the machine and the software, and 'creative editing' is when you start splicing shots together. This is, of course, complete nonsense. There is no such thing as 'creative editing'. It's called editing, and all editing is highly creative.

Think of it like this: Imagine you're a chef and not a director. It's your birthday so you want to celebrate it with friends and family by organising a dinner party and cooking for them. First, you sit down and plan who to invite and what you will eat and drink, and then you make a list of all ingredients you need to buy for the menu. In film terms, this is your prep.

Next, you go to the shops to buy all the ingredients. At the meat counter, you can't find the exact cut of meat you want, so you settle for something similar and decide it will work even better than what you planned to use. In the fruit and vegetable section, you find everything you want, but as an added bonus the tomatoes are absolutely amazing so you buy some extra of them for a side salad, and so on. In film terms, this is your shoot.

So what does that make editing? It's cooking the meal.

Given the same ingredients, a decent chef will cook a decent meal. A good chef will cook a great meal, and a master chef will blow your mind.

A very famous film editor called Thelma Schoonmaker was once asked how it was that such a nice lady could edit Scorsese's violent gangster pictures. She replied with a smile, 'Ah, but they aren't violent until I've edited them.' Thelma has edited almost all Martin Scorsese's movies because they have an 'understanding'. Read about them and you will see why. And, what about Woody Allen and Susan E. Morse? They worked together for 20 years and someone even made a film about their collaboration.

Finding the right editor is as important as finding the right producer. It's a really close working relationship – perhaps the closest of them all. When you have found the 'one', hold on to them! I've worked with many excellent editors over the years (and would love to work with most of them again) but there is one editor called Janey who will always be my number one ever since we worked together for the first time. In the cutting room, we are as one. I know that collaborating with her will always make my film a better film; we think the same way, and she always finds the little things and new options that will look like I planned them but didn't — she did and I always give her the credit for it.

FOOD FOR THOUGHT

The best way to learn how to make a film is by spending time in a cutting room. You will soon realise why statements like 'I was planning to do that shot' and 'My intention was' lose their meaning because in the cutting room, you will only have the footage you have, and that's what you have got to work with. (Think like a chef — if you didn't buy tomatoes you can't make a tomato salad, and now the shops are closed!)

If you need to do pick-up shots or shoot additional material, it is usually your own fault because you didn't do your prep properly (unless, of course, they are shots you had planned but for some reason were unable to do). Learn from your mistakes.

As your career as a director picks up speed, you will find yourself thinking about everything you do as if you were watching the results in the cutting room.

It's a great place to be. The best!

VISUAL EFFECTS (VFX)

There are two VFX scenarios: before and after. 'Before' is when you know there will be visual effects in your film — anything from putting in back-drops, adding extra people in a crowd or adding sections on buildings to creating entire environments (like in *Star Wars*). The sooner you get the VFX people involved, the better. Ideally this happens at the script stage so you can work out what is possible and what you cannot do. As the work progresses, you turn your ideas into more specific plans, and when you have found your studio space and locations, you nail them down into exact plans with storyboards and all.

'After' is when you need to clean up your footage. There might be unwanted road signs and microphones in shot and other visual 'noise' that needs to be removed. This work will not be done until you have finished editing and have locked the picture; but you should always keep your producer and VFX artist up-to-date about things you might need to do, to keep as many options open as possible.

Keep checking with the VFX people and your producer to see if it is an easy job and if you can afford to do it. Or if it's so complicated that the money is better spent re-shooting it, picking another take or simply not using the shot at all. If you wait until you have finished the edit, you are likely to have painted yourself into a corner. And that, my friend, is a place where you don't want to be.

Chapter 20 - THE PRODUCTION MEETING

Some institutions and organisations thrive on endless meetings about this, that and the other. A film production doesn't because there is usually no time to waste. You do have meetings, though, and they're called production meetings.

A production meeting is when the heads of department and other necessary crew members meet up to go through the state of the production. How often you hold them depends on the nature of the film or television programme you are making. Some productions have one every week, others have just two (perhaps one at the start and one just before the shoot), while some television shows I have worked on had none — it was a very well-oiled machine where everybody already knew what everybody else was doing because they'd done it for years. If the crew works well together, less is more.

When you hold a production meeting, the producer or the production manager is in charge. Going around the table, each HoD reports on what's been done and what will be done and presents any possible problems that might affect other HoD's. That's it. It's not a forum for endless and detailed discussion about how to do things. It's about ticking boxes and things off a lists. All problem solving happens on an informal and rolling basis, where people constantly communicate via phone, email or in separate meetings.

In short, the production meeting should be about 'the bigger picture' and the things that will affect everybody. Nothing else. In an ideal world, there will be no surprises, only reassurance that everything is running smoothly, that any problems have been identified and that the solutions are being worked out. This allows you all to get on with your work.

If not, you know you have a communication problem within the team that needs to be identified and resolved very quickly by you and the producer. It could be that some people in the crew don't get on, that someone is not pulling their weight or something as simple as a misunderstanding. This is when your leadership qualities are put to the test. Contrary to beliefs, a good director never assigns blame. A great director would never raises his or her voice at someone else in the crew. Instead, they find a solution to whatever the problem is and present it in a constructive way. By doing so, they will always remain the bigger person, and that is what earns them their respect.

Remember, you're not there to score points or exercise a position of power. You are there to protect the film. The only way to succeed is if you keep everybody on your side.

THE BRICK WALL

Still... at times you will get angry and frustrated when things don't go your way. A good method of dealing with this anger is to disappear around a corner, punch a brick wall until your hand bleeds, stick your hand in your pocket so no one sees the blood and then return to deal with the person or whatever it is that's causing you grief. The pain will override your anger. Anger is very destructive, both during the prep and during the shoot, where you can't afford for even a second to lose your focus on what is important. Try to remain calm at all times. Losing your cool will kick you out of the 'zone' for at least half an hour, and this is something you can't afford.

Chapter 21 - WORKING ON YOUR SCRIPT

While being busy picking your crew, you will also be working on your script. It's important that you can deliver any notes you have to the producer and the script editor (if you have one) within the first couple of days of prep. This will give you time to discuss them and the writer time to make the necessary changes, fix problems or make adjustments that reflect the way you are going to shoot it.

Think carefully about the changes you want to make. The writer has spent a long time writing the script, so be sure you haven't misunderstood his or her intentions before storming in demanding re-writes. Remember you said 'yes' to the script, so you should concentrate on the things that will make it better, not change it into something different.

This is not a book about script writing, so I will not go into any detail about plot structure, turning points and things like that. There are lots of other books about that already.

BUT:

When you work on a script as a director, you will look at it from a slightly different angle than the screen writer. The writer often seeks to answer the question 'how?' when you as a director should be obsessed with the questions 'why?'. Here's your new mantra:

THE FIVE FINGER RULE

Character -> Action -> Plot -> Story -> Script

What does this mean?

Before I explain what it means, I want you to write this your new mantra in neat letters on a piece of paper and stick it on the wall where you sit writing scripts or prepping for a film shoot. If you do it by hand and say it out aloud when you do it that will help you remember it better.

Done it? Good! This is what it means:

1   The CHARACTER is a unique individual with a personality defined by their inheritance (background), experiences and values.

2   The character, when faced with a choice, will only do exactly what he or she would do in any given situation (because of who they are and what they want), and this will result in an ACTION.

An action could be anything from picking your nose, gambling away the family home, blowing up a warehouse to doing nothing at all. You must never allow anyone to do something they wouldn't do just because it solves a story problem or because you can't think of a better way of doing it. You won't get away with it.

3   The string of actions the characters decide on (because of who they are and what they want) will result in a PLOT.

4   That plot can be manipulated by any number of events and obstacles the screen writer decides to throw at the characters, and the result of all this becomes the STORY.

5   The way you decide to tell this story — as a thriller, a horror movie, a film noir or a comedy, to name but a few genres — will result in a SCRIPT.

That's all pretty clear, isn't it? If not, put the book down, take a short pause and read it again. Say it out loud, then spend some time thinking about it, because this is very, very important stuff.

WHY?

Have you ever written a script? If you have, you will know how hard it is. Did you start with a plot or the characters? My guess is that you started with a story and that you ran into problems quite a few times and found yourself in a place where there was no way forward or out. After a few days of despair, you decided to let a character do something they normally wouldn't do. The temptation of an easy way out was overwhelming, particularly if you were under a lot of pressure to finish the script on time. In short, you decided to bend rule number 2.

This is a crime in screen writing, but it is not always done on purpose. Sometimes the writer is not even aware of doing it. However, in nine cases out of ten, it's the reason for why something doesn't work. Your first job as a director is to identify any flaw in the plot or the characters.

Since you didn't write the script, you will have to do the writer's wonderful journey in reverse. You will have to start at point number 5, THE SCRIPT, and work your way back to point number 1, THE CHARACTER, to work out who they really are.

There will be written character descriptions, but reading them is a shortcut I always try to avoid. They could have been produced long before the script was finished, and things will have changed since then. They always do. You are filming the characters in the script, not what the writer's ideas, plans and intentions were for them.

Next, you have to figure out if everything they do makes sense. Read the script again and when you come across something that could potentially be a problem, take a step back and ask yourself what you would have done if you were them (because of who they are and what they want). You may find that the problem is not what you think. It could be the logic of something that happened earlier in the story that needs changing. You will only know this if you have drilled your way through the script all the way down to the essence of who the characters are.

This is not as complicated as it sounds. All you need to do is to understand who they are and what they want.

THE PHILOSOPHER'S STONE

If you do this properly, you will now not just know the characters, you will have done most of your prep for how to direct the actors, because you have the answers to everything they need to know:

Who am I, what do I want, how do I feel about everybody else and why do I do that?

BACK TO THE RE-WRITES

If you're lucky, there will be no changes at all. If you're unlucky, you will end up re-writing the entire script from scratch.

That has happened to me. Seven times.

If you're lucky, the writer will say 'no problem!' If you're unlucky, they will say 'No way. My script is perfect, I'm not changing a single word!' — even if they are wrong.

That has happened to me too.

If you and your best friend the producer agree on what you want to achieve, then they will take care of it and work out the compromise that will make everybody happy.

Chapter 22 - VISUAL STYLE

When I went to film school, there was a media course for teachers being taught in the same building. At the end of their year-long course, they made a short film. They were all very nice and intelligent people who took their work very seriously. I remember sitting in the canteen overhearing a conversation between a group of people from this course, planning the first scene of their film:

```
INT. CANTEEN - DAY

A group of student are sitting at the corner table in the
canteen.

                    STUDENT 1
          Why don't we open with a Hitchcock shot?

                    STUDENT 2
          Great idea, like the one in Psycho!

                    STUDENT 3
          Yeah, that will explain where the story is
          going. Then we cut to a Truffaut-shot, like
          in the final scene of The 400 Blows.

                    STUDENT 2
          Perfect! And we need to get some Tarkovsky-
          like long tracking shots in as well, like in
          Stalker, to make it really beautiful...

All the students smile and nod. Student 3 puts the pen down
and raises his coffee cup to the ceiling. They all do the same
and toast to the success of the film.

                                            FADE OUT
```

I'm not sure that this a completely accurate account, but it makes the point. I picked those references because they probably don't mean anything to you (which is why you should put them on your list of films to watch — they are all amazing films!). Needless to say, they wouldn't have meant anything to whoever watched their film either, because there is no such thing as a Hitchcock shot, a Truffaut shot or a Tarkovsky shot. There are only shots.

Another conversation I overheard in more recent times:

```
INT. PUB - NIGHT

A group of hipsters are sitting at a table in the far corner
of the pub.

                    FILM STUDENT 1
          I just saw the latest Wes Anderson film! Let's
          shoot it like that.

                    FILM STUDENT 2
          But we're making a horror film...?

                    FILM STUDENT 1
          Yeah, I know, but I just luuurve his visual
          style.

                                               CUT TO:
```

THE TRUTH

If you want to make a truly beautiful film, the way to shoot it must spring from your script, your characters and your story.

ANOTHER TRUTH

There is no such thing as a beautiful shot. There is only the shot that is appropriate for a particular moment, and that's what makes it beautiful. Full stop.

Okay, you say, everything has been done before! Well, that's what Charlie Chaplin, Ingmar Bergman, Alfred Hitchcock, Francois Truffaut, Andrei Tarkovsky, Wes Anderson and the Cohen Brothers thought before they got started. They all watched a lot of movies and learned about all the possibilities. Then, because of who they are, they did things their own way and what they did ended up being their style.

Let me make a parallel to music. When a musician (jazz musicians in particular) set out to learn his or her craft, they usually practise and learn their favourite performers' solos by heart. Not to play them in public (most famous solos will be instantly recognised by the audience and they will be written off as a copy-cats), but as a way of assimilating what the great players did, master their techniques and put it in the melting pot of their minds in search of their own voice. Influenced a bit by this and a little bit by that, yes, but never an impersonator.

This applies to you too. Watch loads of movies, assimilate your favourite director's style if you like, but never, ever make a film 'in the style of' or a pastiche or a parody. It will never look as good, it will always look cheap and your film will fall flat on its face. Your favourite director arrived at their particular style because of who they are, what they knew at the time and what they had experienced in life. This is what made them tell a story in the way they did. You should do the same.

YOUR VISUAL STYLE

You will work out what the visual style will be by looking at your story. Ask yourself the following questions: is it fast moving or slow? Is it frantic or poetic? Funny or scary? Reflective or argumentative? Do you want the audience to be 'inside the character's experience' or should they come across as being distant? Is it highly stylised or hyper realistic? Whatever the answer, your camera work and editing should reflect this.

Here's another parallel from the wonderful world of music: the opera. Opera is what everybody used to go to before a guy called Soren invented the cinema. It was the place to hang out with your friends, eat, drink and be entertained. The music was usually pretty good too.

Do you know what an aria is? It's when a character in an opera sings a solo accompanied by the orchestra. The way it works is that the singer sings the words and the orchestra plays along, illustrating what the character is really feeling. So if a soprano sings a really calm and sweet tune while the music played by the orchestra is full of sweeping, dramatic scales and trembling notes in the bass, you can assume that she's pretending to be happy when, in reality, she's is quite upset with something. You don't have to understand the plot or speak the language she is singing in. The orchestra is illustrating the underlying meaning — or what is called the subtext.

SUBTEXT

Translating this into images, the visuals should do what the orchestra is doing in the opera. They should show us and articulate the underlying meaning of a scene and the nature of the film. When watching a clip from a movie, you can always tell what kind of film it is by the way it's been shot. Enter the genre (or 'type of film')

GENRE

There are a number of genres, and you have probably seen them all: action, thriller, comedy, horror, film noir, etc. They all come with expectations and have a well established visual grammar.

Action: Fast or very fast editing.
Thriller: Lots of close-ups picking out details to create suspense.
Comedy: Works best in medium and wide shots.
Horror: Close-ups and surprise cuts.
Film Noir: Often slowly paced and set at night, with lots of deep shadows.

If you decided that your film belongs to one of those genres, then your choice of visual style and the overall feeling of the film has been narrowed down. This doesn't mean you can't mix and match and break existing rules, but it is a good starting point for the overall process.

Chapter 23 - WORKING OUT YOUR SHOTS

The next step is to reduce all the endless shot options, ideas and possibilities into camera set-ups and decide exactly what you are going to do on the day.

This is a painful process (see appendix II). You will have a vast number of dreamlike images, pictures and shots floating around in your imagination. Some of them will be wide and tight at the same time. Some of them are never-ending developing shots, others will be shots using 'rubber lenses' that can magically look around corners. There will be cameras flying through the air.

You can see them all in your inner eye, but the moment you try putting them down on paper, they become very elusive.

So, you ask, why not just wait until the shoot and decide then? The answer is that by then it's too late. Aha, you say, I've seen Steven Spielberg in behind-the-scenes footage wandering around with his viewfinder working out angles...! To which the answer is: He is far ahead of you in his film making skills. He is not making up shots as he goes along, he is just fine-tuning his ideas with some input from his DoP and operator.

The point of making shot plans is that it forces you to explore your script in a way that will help you understand how it works and what is actually important. What I'm going to explain now is not a secret but a foolproof method of how to do it.

TENNIS, ANYONE?

Have you ever watched a game of tennis? If you have, lean back and recall with your inner eye a good game you watched. Perhaps a Wimbledon final between Federer and Djokovic. If you have never seen a game of tennis, this is how it works:

First guy serves. Second guy sees where the ball is going to go and, during the short run to meet it, makes a quick decision on how to best return the ball. To the left? To the right? To the centre? First guy is waiting in anticipation. When the ball heads back towards the net, he or she has to make a split second decision and run to where he thinks it's going to go. If he guessed right, he will return it to a place on the court he thinks is the most difficult for the other player to reach. This will go on until one of them misses or when one guy hits a ball so hard the second guy can't reach it. The obvious observation is that every time one of the players hits the ball, the ball changes direction.

This can be applied to analysing a scene.

Have you ever watched a scene in a movie? This is how it works: A scene begins. It goes on for a bit, then something unexpected happens that makes the scene go off in a new direction. It could be when someone opens a drawer in a desk and finds something unexpected inside, or when a husband tells his wife over a glass of wine that he is actually her brother. Those moments are called 'beats' and they are very important.

Chapter 24 - THE BEAT

A beat in a scene is the equivalent of a tennis player hitting the ball to make it change direction. Or when a wanderer comes to a crossroad. A beat is a point in a scene when a character is faced with something that forces him or her to make a decision. Whether they are big or small decisions doesn't matter — they are still decisions and they are all important.

Your job as a director is to know where and what every single one of those beats are. If you do, you will understand what is going on in the scene and why your characters are behaving the way they do. This will help you understand what is going on in every character's mind at any given moment in the film. In short, you will know what to tell the actors when you direct them.

There can be any number of beats in a scene. The last beat is usually the most important because it will propel us into the next scene.

YOUR ROAD TO HAPPINESS

1 Work out the beats in the scene.

2 Identify the most important beat. In tennis terms, it's the winning ball.

3 Work out the best place for the camera to be to catch the most important beat and — Bingo! — chances are that you have just found a 'one-shot-solution' for the whole scene.

Remember that you can let the actors move around to manoeuvre themselves into position! The most common way of making a long dialogue scene more interesting is to have the characters walking towards the camera and stop close to the lens to deliver the punchline.

4 Make a list of all the other possible shots.

5 Look at your schedule and figure out how many of them you will have time to do. Decide which shots you think are the most important ones to do the scene justice.

6 Make your shot list, draw your story boards or make your floor plans.

FILM IS VISUAL STORYTELLING

My rule of thumb is to cut or move the camera to mark a beat but never go back to the same shot twice. Why? It's simple. If something has changed in the scene, the images on the screen should reflect that. If you cut back to the same shot again and again (like that wide shot you made for 'safety'), the underlying point you will make visually is that nothing has changed.

The exception to this is of course in dialogue scenes where you will cut back and forth between characters. A way to mark a beat is then to cut to a tighter or wider shot. Tighter if the stakes have been upped for that character and wider if they have been left behind in the emotional race.

TIME TO APPLY IT

On the next page, you'll find a short scene. Read it a few times and work out the following two ways of how you would plan to shoot it:

1 The one-shot option.

2 The as-many-shots-as-you-like option.

I will give my version in the following chapter. Try not look at it before you have come up with your own solution!

Chapter 25 - SAMPLE SCENE

INT. DRAWING ROOM - DAY

Sherlock Holmes is sitting on a chair in his room playing the violin. There is a knock on the door. He finishes the piece he is playing.

     SHERLOCK
  Come in!

Mrs Hudson steps in through the door. Sherlock looks up. Mrs Hudson continues into the room and sits on the chair opposite him.

     SHERLOCK (CONT'D)
  Why are you here?

     MRS HUDSON
  You sent for me.

     SHERLOCK
  Did I?

     MRS HUDSON
  Didn't you?

A beat.

     SHERLOCK
  Look in the drawer over there.

     MRS HUDSON
  Why?

She hesitates, then she stands and walks over to the chest of drawers she passed on her way in.

She pulls out the top left drawer. Inside the drawer is a small box. She picks it up and opens it. Inside the box is a diamond ring. For a moment she holds her breath. Then her stern face dissolves into a big smile.

     MRS HUDSON (CONT'D)
  Oh, Sherlock.

She turns around. Sherlock smiles and rises from his chair as Mrs Hudson runs straight into his arms.

THE END

Chapter 26 - WORKING OUT THE BEATS

Have you figured out a way to shoot it? Did you find it easy or difficult?
Let's start by working out what the beats are:

READY, STEADY, GO!

1   Is Sherlock Holmes playing the violin a beat?
    No, that is what is going on in the room when we start the scene.

2   Is someone knocking on the door a beat?
    Ask yourself if it changes the direction of the scene. If Sherlock had stopped playing straight away, it would be, but at the moment, it is just a noise. As far as we know, he could have been playing for hours while someone was standing outside knocking on the door all this time and this could go on forever. There is nothing indicating he has heard it. He could, as far as we know, be deaf! So no, it's not a beat because it doesn't change the direction of the scene.

3   When Sherlock stops playing, is that a beat?
    No. He has come to the end of the piece, so he would stop.

4   Is shouting 'Come in' a beat?
    No. It only informs us that he heard someone knocking and he is still alone in the room.

5   Is Mrs Hudson stepping into the room a beat?
    Definitely. She could have decided not to come in. There are now two people in the room and that breaks the status quo. From now on, a whole range of new options open up for the scene.

6   Is Mrs Hudson walking across the room and sitting down on the chair a beat?
    No. She is already in the room. If she has come to listen to Sherlock play, she is just finding herself a better place to do this. Next up: the dialogue.

7   Is Sherlock's question 'Why are you here?' a beat?
    No. It is a natural development of the scene, and so is the rest of the dialogue.

8. Is 'A beat' a beat?

    Not always. It depends on what happens in that beat (because something always does; it's never just a pause). In this case, having read the rest of the scene, I came to the conclusion that this is where Sherlock decides to go ahead with his plan to ask Mrs Hudson to marry him. He could have changed his mind and asked her to bring him a cup of tea instead.

9. Is Sherlock telling her to look in the drawer 'over there' a beat?

    No it isn't, but Mrs Hudson's decision to get up is. She could have said no, and if she had, that would have been a beat, too.

10. Is walking up to the chest of drawers and opening the top drawer a beat?

    No, she is still executing her decision to do what Sherlock has asked her to do, so it is just a natural development of the scene. If she had hesitated and decided not to open the drawer that would have been a beat.

11. Is seeing the small box a beat?

    No, but her decision to pick it up is, because she could have chosen not to.

12. Is her opening the small box a beat?

    Yes. It's a mystery box. Whatever is in there will probably change the course of the scene. If it had been empty that would have been a surprise and that would have been a beat too.

13. Is Mrs Hudson seeing the diamond ring a beat?

    Yes. When Mrs Hudson (and we as an audience) realises what the ring means, she will come to the conclusion that Sherlock is proposing to her.

14. Is Mrs Hudson and Sherlock Holmes embracing a beat?

    No, but I'd guess there are two hearts beating pretty quickly at this point! The embrace is just confirming their smiles of happiness.

That's it. These are our beats, and I hope it all makes sense to you. Let's list them:

THE BEATS

1. Mrs Hudson acting on her decision to step into the room.
2. Sherlock deciding to ask her to do something.
3. Mrs Hudson deciding to do it.
4. Mrs Hudson deciding to pick up the box.
5. Mrs Hudson's decision to open the box.
6. Mrs Hudson realising that Sherlock wants to marry her.

As you can see, following the initial shock of someone stepping inside the room, every single beat is when someone has to a make a decision. At every point, each of them could have decided to do something different, but by doing what they decided to do, they changed the course of the scene.

THE MOST IMPORTANT BEAT

So, what is the most important beat in the scene? I'd say it's beat number 6. Sherlock Holmes asking Mrs Hudson to marry him is not only a scene changer, it's a life changer. I would go as far as to claim it is one of the most important beats in the whole Sherlock Holmes Saga!

THE ONE-SHOT SOLUTION

If we can agree on beat number 6 being the most important (where Mrs Hudson realises that Sherlock wants to marry her), our next task is to decide where the camera should be to catch it.

Where will she be in the room? Well, if she passed the chest of drawers on her way in, we can assume that this is placed near the door, that Sherlock will be sitting at the opposite end of the room (by the window perhaps) and that she will be standing with her back to Sherlock when she opens the box.

If we put the camera behind this chest of drawers, we will see the whole first part of the scene play out in a wider two shot, and when she walks up to the chest of drawers, she will walk into a close up of her face as she opens the box. We will be on her face when she smiles, and when she turns away from us to look at Sherlock, it will almost be like cutting to her point of view of him before she runs into his arms.

The only beat we will miss out on is beat number 1 (when she steps into the room) but I think we can live with that because we will find out who was knocking on the door the moment she walks into the room and sits down.

APRIL FOOL

Most inexperienced directors will point to words in the dialogue when asked about the beats in a scene. When preparing, they will also spend a lot of time working out exactly how to say a line and later, when directing the actors, point out to them how they should stress one word and not another. This is a complete waste of time. If the actor is clear about what the character is thinking in that moment, they will say the words pitch perfect.

If you look at the scene again, you will understand what I mean when I tell you that the only line of dialogue that needs to be spoken is the one with an exclamation mark: 'Come in!' All the other lines can be done with looks.

It's never the words that steers a scene. It's the thought process behind them.

Chapter 27 - SHARING YOUR IDEAS

There are three basic ways of presenting your shots:

1. Shot lists
2. Storyboards
3. Floor plans

SHOT LIST

A shot list is exactly what it says. It's a list of shots. Nothing more, nothing less. The good thing about having a shot list is that you have decided on how many shots you need and what size they are, but that's the only information the rest of the crew can draw from it.

So, the shot list version of our one-shot solution would look something like this:

Sc 101 INT. SHERLOCK HOLMES STUDY - DAY

1/ Wide shot of the room. 24 mm lens.

That's it. Let's take a look at option two, the storyboard:

STORYBOARD

A storyboard is a set of drawings of the shots you are planning to do — shot by shot — as individual pictures. If you are a good at drawing and this is done well, it can be a thing of beauty in itself. The Japanese director Kurosawa spent a long time before each film he made painting the entire movie in exquisite water colours that are today worth a fortune.

If you are not good at drawing, but have some money to spend, you can hire a storyboard artist to do it for you. Or, you can visit your locations with a friend or a crew member, stage the scenes, take pictures with a digital camera and print the shots.

As you can see, each moment is captured by a picture, and as a viewer, you can tell what the scene in going to look like. But it is still pretty limited in information. Why? Because it doesn't tell you anything about what's going on outside the frame.

So, what does our third option, the floor plans have to offer?

FLOOR PLANS

A floor plan is when you first make a drawing of the location from a bird's eye point of view — like a map — and then mark out people, how they move, important objects, etcetera and show where the camera is going to be with the use of simple symbols.

This is what our Sherlock Holmes scene would look like:

SHERLOCK HOLMES STUDY

1/ Sherlock playing (1) -> Mrs Hudson (1) enter and sits opposite him (2) -> Mrs Hudson walks up to chest of drawers (3) -> opens drawer and finds box with ring -> Sherlock rises (2) -> Mrs Hudson runs towards him (4) and they embrace.

As you can see, the shot list and the storyboard are pretty straightforward, but they don't give a fraction of the information you will share by making a floorplan. This is what your crew can work out from a quick glance at it:

1. The Art Department can see exactly where you want the furniture.
2. The Art Department can see what other parts of the room will be in shot and need to be dressed.
3. The DoP can see where the windows are and work out where to place the lights.
4. The gaffer can see the potential problem of the camera looking straight at two windows and can prepare to put up filters if it is a sunny day.
5. The 1st AC can work out how and when they will pull focus.
6. The 2nd AC can take a good guess at what lenses you are going to use.
7. The Sound Department can work out where the boom operator should be.
8. Continuity can work out where to put the monitor so it doesn't have to be moved every time the camera moves (if you're doing more than one shot).
9. The grip can tell straight away if you're using a tripod or tracks.

Amazing, isn't it? Imagine the amount of time this will save you and your crew. Everybody will know exactly what you are going to do without you having to explain anything. This will buy you time to do your own job properly: to work with the actors, get the performances right and make the film a better film.

Another additional benefit of the floor plan is that you've already created an image in people's minds of what the scene will look like when it's being shot. (I admit that a story board does that, too, but why draw six pictures when you can draw one?) You can take the same floor plan and drop the scene into a different location. When arriving on set, your crew members can work out possible advantages of perhaps moving the chairs around in this or that direction because they can see straight away how it would affect any other camera set-ups.

MY ADVICE

1 Make floor plans with a shot list or description written on the same page.

> There are many ways of doing this:
> You can draw them with a pen on a piece of paper.
> You can do what I do and make them in Photoshop using a tablet and pen.
> You can use one of many purpose-made computer software programs or apps.

2 When you have finished the floor plans, give them to your 1st AD who will photocopy them and hand them out to the crew. This is important: always make sure that everybody gets a copy so you know they all have the same information!

3 Make a storyboard for a sequence when you need to communicate your ideas with visual effects (VFX) artists when they are going to add things to an image in post-production, or when you are doing a stunt and need to show or explain to a stunt coordinator exactly what you expect to see or happen (more about that below).

Ok, so we found the single shot solution that is pretty satisfactory. Let's look at what shots we can add to this and how to work them out by looking at the beats.

Let's say we want Sherlock to look up at Mrs Hudson when she enters the room. The master shot is good for this. Where shall we put the camera to see her reaction best? Before we can decide this, we need cover a technical element of film making by taking a look at the line and establish what it is.

Chapter 28 - THE LINE

The line is the most basic and fundamental element in visual storytelling. It's something so simple and logical that most directors will get it wrong from time to time and, when they do, they get so confused that the scripty has to step in and sort it all out.

The easiest way of defining the line is to look at two people sitting opposite each other talking. The line here is the invisible axis between them and what they are looking at (in this case, another person). Some people think of it as a piece of string.

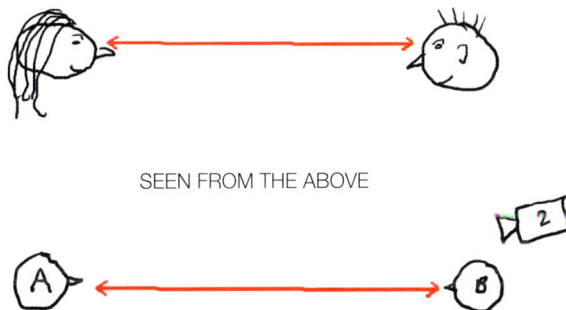

So why is this important? Well, it informs you about where to put the camera when you film the dialogue. If you want them to look at each other, then the two camera positions must be on the same side of this imagined line, like this:

If you imagine what Mr B will look like in the shot from camera position 1, he will look from right to left in the frame. Ms A will look from left to right in camera position 2, like this:

They appear to be looking at each other. If you keep the camera on this side of the line, we will understand that he is sitting to right of her and she is sitting to the left of him.

If you move the camera to the other side of the line in both shots, it will look like this:

Ms A and Mr B have swapped sides, but they are still looking at each other.

CROSSING THE LINE (1)

This is an expression you will have heard before: 'You can't shoot it from there, you're crossing the line!' Why can't you? Well, take a look at what happens if you move the second camera position across the line for the shot of Ms A.

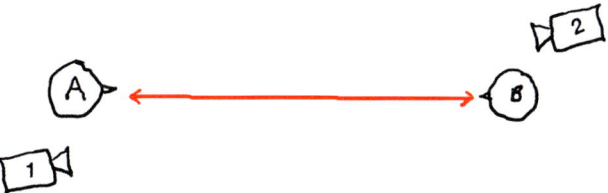

The two shots will now look like this:

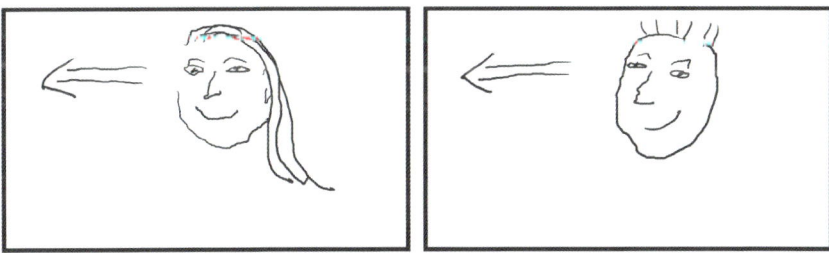

Even if they are still looking at each other in real life, the camera will tell a different story. It now appears as if they are both looking at someone sitting to their left, which is very confusing, even if you established how they are sitting with a two-shot at the top of the scene. It will appear as if they are jumping around.

RULE OF THUMB

Pay attention now because this is very important, and it's the only thing you need to know: it's how the characters relate to the the camera that decides where they are in relation to each other in the room, not where they are in a physical reality.

If you don't believe me, take a look at this:

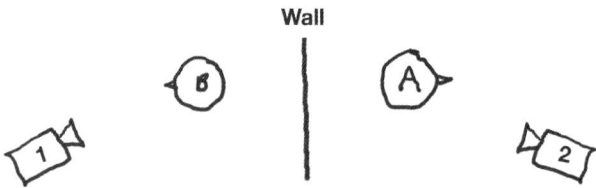

Ms A and Mr B are now in two separate rooms. They can't even see each other, let alone look each other in the eyes. But when you look at the shots, the result will be this:

Chapter 29 - THE MULTIPLE SHOT VERSION

Let's go back to our scene with Sherlock Holmes and work out what other shots we want to do and how to do them guided by our new knowledge about the line. Is there a line in camera position 1 (Pos 1) when Sherlock is sitting alone playing the violin? If he is playing with his eyes closed, the answer is no.

If he looks up at the score on the music stand and you want to cut to a shot of the printed music, then yes. The line is between him and what he is looking at.

When he looks up at Mrs Hudson stepping into the room, there's a line between them (A).

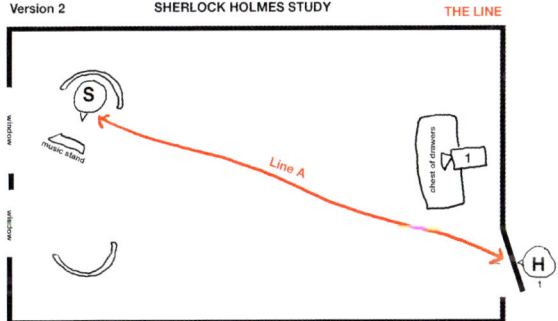

So where shall we put the camera to get a shot of Mrs Hudson? Assuming we keep our master shot (the one-shot solution), we have to work out in what direction Sherlock will look when she steps inside the door. Imagine what the camera in position 1 will see:

The door is to the left of camera, so Sherlock will be looking right to left at Mrs Hudson. If we want Mrs Hudson to look back at him from there, then the next camera position must be on the same side of Line A. Let's put it near Sherlock pointing towards the door and let Mrs Hudson enter!

Before you move the camera to the next position, you could shoot a close-up of Sherlock from this position, too, if you adjust Mrs Hudson's activity a bit to the left.

CAMERA POSITION 2

When she stops inside the door, she will looking at him from left to right. As she moves through the room to the chair, the line 'follows' her and Line A ends up as Line B, where she will still look at him from left to right.

From this angle, we can cover all the beats 1, 2 and 3 (when she decides to get up), but also beats 4, 5 (where we will be behind her, but that is what Sherlock would see from where he is sitting) and final important beat 6 (where she spins around)

Pos 2 is, in other words, another possible one-shot solution as it covers all the beats.

If you keep the shot wide-ish (ending up with an MCU when she is sits on the chair), you should shoot an additional close-up of her, too, from the same position. It will only take the time it takes to change the lens and do it again.

Our shot list so far:

Pos 1	Shot 1	Wide Master
	Shot 2	CU Sherlock when Mrs Hudson stand by the chest of drawers.
Pos 2	Shot 3	Pan/MCU Mrs Hudson enters -> sits -> up to chest of drawers
	Shot 4	CU Mrs Hudson dialogue -> up to chest of drawers -> the end

CAMERA POSITION 3

Our next camera position is the reverse shot of Sherlock for the dialogue. This should be done with the same lenses and with the camera at exactly the same angle, height and distance from him as it was from her for the two shots to match.

Pos 3	Shot 5	MCU Sherlock -> Mrs Hudson sits -> gets up again
	Shot 6	CU Sherlock -> Mrs Hudson site -> gets up again

Now you may ask, why don't I stay on Sherlock through the rest of the scene from camera position 3? Take another look at the plan.

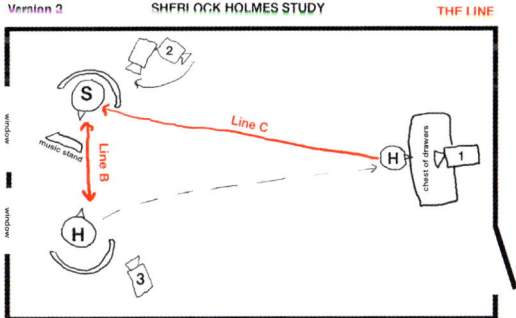

When Mrs Hudson moves across the room to the chest of drawers, camera positions 2 and 3 are suddenly on different sides of the new line (Line C)!

WHICH SIDE SHALL I CHOOSE?

If you want to continue using the master (Pos 1), where Sherlock is on the right side of Mrs Hudson when she is standing straight in front of the camera, you'll find that he has already been firmly established as looking at her from right to left in the frame.

If you panned with Mrs Hudson from the chair to the chest of drawers in Pos 2, she will look at him from left to right in the frame when she turns, meaning they look at each other. Both angles are still working.

But: If you were to cut to a shot of Sherlock from Pos 3 now, he would be looking from left to right in the frame, just like Mrs Hudson, so they would not be looking at each other. In short, Pos 3 is over and done within the second she passes in front of camera. Cut!

HANG ON...!

Yes. You could shoot the rest of the scene from the 'south' side of the line where Pos 3 is, but I wouldn't. The angle is not that great for Sherlock watching Mrs Hudson at the other end of the room (he is in profile), and you would have to sacrifice Pos 2 for the rest of the scene. Pos 2 is already working well by covering the entire scene. Staying on the 'south' side of the line would mean that we would have to re-light the room and move the acripty's monitor around (it's placed in the top right-hand corner of the room, which is the only part of the location we haven't seen yet), and to me, that all sounds like a lot of unnecessary work and a waste of time.

Let's stay on the 'north' side; it's the smoothest way of doing it.

CAMERA POSITION 4

If we agree that the first three camera positions take care of the main mechanics of the scene, let's see if there are any details we want to pick up on to enhance the drama... Let's look in the drawer!

We have our close-up of Mrs Hudson already in Pos 1, so looking at what is in the drawer would be her POV:

If she is looking in the drawer to her left, you will put the camera in Pos 4A.
If she is looking in the drawer to her right, you will put the camera in Pos 4B.

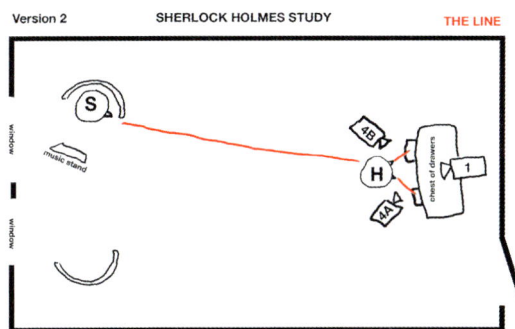

That should cover the stuff in the drawers, and with that, you will have a perfectly functioning scene covering all the beats in four camera set-ups and seven shots. Not bad.

Our new shot list looks like this:

Pos 1	Shot 1	Wide Master
	Shot 2	CU Sherlock looking towards the chest of drawers.
Pos 2	Shot 3	Pan/MCU Mrs Hudson enters -> sits -> exit to chest of drawers.
	Shot 4	CU Mrs H dialogue -> Pan up to chest of drawers -> the end
Pos 3	Shot 5	MCU Sherlock -> Mrs Hudson sits -> gets up again
	Shot 6	CU Sherlock -> Mrs Hudson site -> gets up again
Pos 4	Shot 7	CU object in drawer.

That should cover it.

I STILL HAVE TIME TO SPEND

If you do have more time to spend, let's take a look look at some moments that could be enhanced. The first must be when both of them look over to the chest of drawers and Mrs Hudson is deciding to follow Sherlock's instruction. You could use Pos 1 for this.

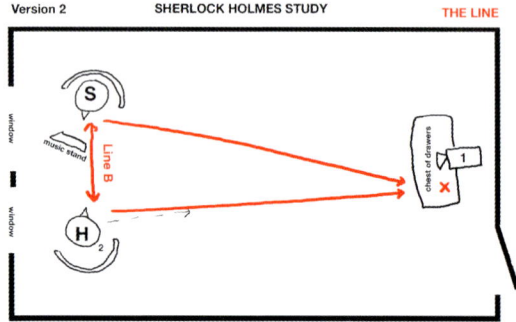

If you shoot the close-up of Sherlock (shot 2), you could have done do the same CU of Mrs Hudson when you were in this position, catching her looking at the drawer, then back at Sherlock. As she stands to walk up to the chest of drawers, you can pan to Sherlock.

Pos 1   Shot 8   CU Mrs Hudson -> Pan to Sherlock as she rises.

If you want a more intimate shot of the hug at the end of the scene, you can go on a tighter lens and catch that moment from this position, too:

Pos 1   Shot 9   MCU Sherlock spinning Mrs Hudson around and kissing her.

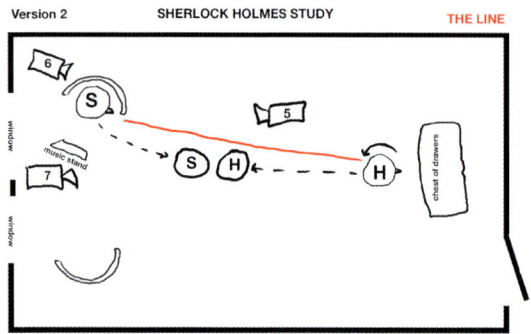

CAMERA POSITION 5

Perhaps you want a different close-up of Sherlock watching Mrs Hudson at the chest of drawers than the one you get from Pos 1? If you do, put the camera anywhere between her and Sherlock looking back at him.

Pos 5　　　　Shot 10　CU Sherlock watching Mrs Hudson

CAMERA POSITION 6

Maybe you want to enhance Sherlock's presence when he is watching her searching the drawer, using a stronger POV shot (than that of Pos 2)? You could go over his shoulder and change the perspective of the scene over to him in combination with shot 10.

Pos 6　　　　Shot 11　Sherlock POV of Mrs Hudson

CAMERA POSITION 7

And if you want a fresh new shot for the end hug, I would suggest raising the camera to eye-level in Pos 7 and shooting this in two sizes: a wide and an MCU of the two together.

CROSSING THE LINE II

I mentioned before that crossing the line can be used as a tool to mark a great change. There's an opportunity to do this here. When Mrs Hudson is going through the drawer, you can use the crossing the line on purpose to unsettle the viewer. Mrs Hudson's actions by the drawer and finding the box happens somewhat in isolation. She is in a world of her own — and so is Sherlock. He is waiting in anticipation.

If you were to jump Pos 5 and 6 to the other side of the line, you would underline this by unsettling the audience in the way Sherlock is unsettled by the uncertainty of the outcome. It would not be 'confusing' (we know the room pretty well by now), but it would underline the dramatic moment by switching the entire perspective away from Mrs Hudson to Sherlock's.

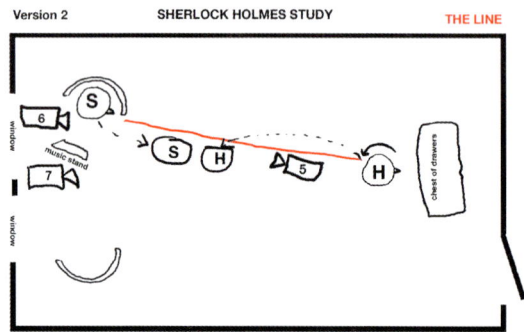

The extended shot list would look something like this:

Pos 1	Shot 1	Wide Master
	Shot 2	CU Sherlock looking towards the chest of drawers.
	Shot 8	CU Mrs Hudson -> Pan to Sherlock as she rises.
	Shot 9	MCU Sherlock spinning Mrs Hudson around and kissing her.
Pos 2	Shot 3	Pan/MCU Mrs Hudson enters -> sits -> exit to chest of drawers.
	Shot 4	CU Mrs H dialogue -> Pan up to chest of drawers -> the end
Pos 3	Shot 5	MCU Sherlock -> Mrs Hudson sits -> gets up again
	Shot 6	CU Sherlock -> Mrs Hudson sits -> gets up again
Pos 4	Shot 7	CU object in drawer.
Pos 5	Shot 10	CU Sherlock watching Mrs Hudson
Pos 6	Shot 11	Sherlock POV of Mrs Hudson
Pos 7	Shot 12	Wide + MCU Sherlock spinning Mrs Hudson around and kissing her.

TRACKS

I haven't suggested using any tracks in this scene. If you want to do some (and have the time to do it), let me suggest a formula for how you should do them in an intimate scene like this to enhance the beats.

Make them little ones and pick the moments carefully. A track in an overall static scene tends to be explosive. This is how you do it and what they mean:

Example 1:

Sherlock says: 'Look in the drawer over there.' Just as he finishes saying the line (not before), you start tracking in on Mrs Hudson's face. This move means she's thinking about it. When the camera stops, it means she has decided what to do. She waits a very brief moment, then she gets up from the chair.

Example 2:

Mrs Hudson has just opened the little box and seen the diamond ring. Wait for a beat, then cut to Sherlock and track in on his face. This will enhance his expectation, waiting for Mrs Hudson's reaction... When the camera stops, cut back to Mrs Hudson, waiting for a beat before she spins around to look at him. Cut back to him looking at her, then cut back to her breaking into a smile.

As you can see, the little tracks here are showing us that the characters are thinking about something, making that thought process more dramatic.

AN IMPORTANT NOTE

This is just one way of shooting the scene. I could think of another ten, depending on what the rest of the film looks like. The shot plans are done to illustrate the basics, showing you a very straightforward way of thinking by addressing the simple underlying logic of the beats. That's all. Go experiment!

SHOOTING ORDER

Your 1st AD will plan the shoot doing all the shots looking in one direction before turning the set around. If the scene you shot before this is only looking towards the windows, he or she will start shooting this scene looking that way. If that same scene is to be shot after this, you will start shooting in the direction of the chest of drawers. Daylight conditions and actors availability will decide.

Chapter 30 - STUNTS

Are there any stunts in your film? It's a good question because the first thing you think when you hear the word 'stunt' is someone falling off a rooftop or crashing a car at high speed. The reality is somewhat less dramatic.

Any situation where an actor can get hurt should be dealt with as a stunt. It can be little actions like tripping over when running in a forest, or falling off a bike. However small the risk involved, this needs to be eliminated so it can be done in a safe way that will make it work in the film. When an actor feels comfortable about doing something, it will look good. If they're not, however simple the action may be, they will hesitate and will not do it in a convincing way.

Films are made during prep, so if you have any doubts, bring on the stunt coordinator.

THE STUNT COORDINATOR

Most people think it's the stuntman or stuntwoman who works out a stunt, but it's not. It's the stunt coordinator. He or she is usually a very experienced stunt person who knows a lot of stunt actors and knows who will be the best to pick for the job (skills and looks, if there is one to be had). There are around 600 registered Stunt persons in the UK, out of which 60 do most of the jobs.

First you organise a meeting with the stunt coordinator, the designer (they usually need to build or design something for the event) and the 1st AD (who is responsible for health and safety on the set and who will go to prison if something he or she didn't anticipate goes wrong). If the DoP and the producer are around, invite them, too.

Next you go through the script and explain the bits you are unsure about, what you want to happen and what you want to see. There is always more than one way to do a stunt, so when you have finished, the stunt coordinator will ask you a whole lot of questions. They need to understand the nature of the story, the characters involved, the overall feeling of the film and the visual style, to help narrowing down the options to get it right.

Let's use an example. Say that a character in your film is going to fall off a bike. First you will have to decide which element of 'falling off a bike' is the most important.

1   Is it the action that makes them lose balance (someone bumping into them)?
2   Is it the anticipation of them falling?
3   Is it the moment when they are finally falling over?
4   Is it the moment when they hit the ground?

That's four different stunts.

If it is an action film, you will probably make every moment the most important moment and it will be a complicated sequence to shoot.

If it is a comedy and it's the anticipation of someone falling off or hitting something, you might find that it isn't a stunt at all, just someone riding past the camera followed by the sound of a crash followed by a shot of them on the ground and getting up.

When you decided on the best solution, the stunt coordinator will help you break down the action into necessary shots and work out a way of doing them safely.

ACTOR OR STUNT PERSON?

Before they can decide if you can use your actor or not, they need to know who the actor is, talk to them and, in some cases, meet them first. Most actors' CVs will say they are good at stage fighting, or that they do contact sports, parachute jumping, horse riding and climbing. You should know by now that assumption is the mother of all disasters. They could have done stage fighting or any of the above once when at drama school 5 to 25 years ago. Ask them, then check again!

If the stunt coordinator is happy with who they find, then go for it. They should be there on the day to make sure it will be safe. If they insist you need a stuntman but you can't afford one, you will either work out a cheaper solution or re-think the sequence.

IS IT WORTH IT?

Remember you are the Protector of the Film! If an actor gets injured, twists an ankle or a wrist, you will have compromised the rest of the shoot.

FOOD FOR THOUGHT

I learned everything I know about stunts from a great man called Peter Diamond (*Indiana Jones, Star Wars* etc) He had a simple rule of thumb: Keep it simple! Less is more. If you over-complicate it, you will draw attention to a stunt being — a stunt.

If you are doing a big stunt, you should insist on a special recce to the location(s) with the stunt coordinator, the producer, the 1 AD, designer, DoP and location manager. They will all have input and a say in what you will do.

Filming stunts is very time consuming and, frankly, pretty boring except for that brief exciting moment of danger. However safe it looks, make sure you get it right the first time. If you have to repeat it even once, you have doubled the chance of something going wrong. Even the best laid plans...

Chapter 31 - REHEARSALS

Rehearsals are becoming a thing of the past — at least if you're making television drama. That doesn't stop you from insisting on having them. When I started directing, you would get at least a couple of days or sometimes up to a week to rehearse the actors. It's a very good investment in the film. The time spent rehearsing will pay off big time when you start shooting.

In my experience, rehearsals are quite 'theatrical' in the sense that you spend a lot of time just talking about the character(s), scenes and the story rather than practising them. If you, from where you are sitting now, can see the 5 FINGER POINT mantra I asked you to write on a piece of paper and put on your wall, you will understand why. Rehearsals are about digging deep into the characters so the actor understands everything about them. Any actor will look at the part from their own perspective, not yours. They will see it through the filter of their own experiences of life and feed this into their character to make him or her three dimensional.

LISTEN CAREFULLY

Rehearsals are a time where you start out by listening very carefully to what the actor believes the part to be. Don't interrupt, just listen. If they have it completely wrong (which they rarely do), you need to know this before you start talking. You will discover new shades you hadn't seen before. Even if they don't chime with your view, this is the only starting point. By listening, then adding thoughts, making them feel your ideas are their own, you develop a trust and a shorthand between you. Things will happen and anecdotes will be told that you later that will refer to and use as a directing tool. In short, there's no technique involved here, only a meeting of minds.

Chapter 32 - THE TECH RECCE

Tech recce is short for 'technical reconnaissance', which is much longer, harder to pronounce and trickier to spell.

The tech recce is 'a day out' when key personnel of the crew go to look at all the locations together AS A GROUP. This is very important. You do it within a week before the shoot.

The location manager is responsible for the day. If the locations you are going to visit are spread around, he or she will probably rent a minibus to ship you all around.

On that bus will be you and the producer, the HoDs and some of the key crew members they need to bring along, like the art director, the gaffer, the grip and the 2nd AD. If you are doing any stunts, the stunt coordinator should be there too - unless you've done a separate recce with them already. Make-up and costume usually stay behind.

PRE-TECH RECCE INFO

Before you set off, the location manager will have sent out a recce schedule outlining where you are going and when, where you are going to have lunch and sometimes even a menu so you can pre-order your food (which saves you time).

The 1st AD will hand out a pre-recce schedule (a copy of the schedule as it stands on that day) and your shot plans (if you have finished them).

THE ACID TEST

When you arrive at a location, everybody gathers around the 1st AD, who explains what the location is, what days you will be filming there and what scenes you are going to shoot. Then it's over to you.

You walk and talk the crew through the staging and the shots, showing and explaining exactly what you want to do where and how. Each crew member will take notes and ask relevant questions about things that will affect them and their department. You will discuss every foreseeable problem and decide how to solve them.

1   The grip will check the floor in a house or the ground outside it to see if it is solid enough to carry a track or if you need to put down boards first as support.

2   The gaffer will check the electric wiring and work out if there is enough power available for the lighting, or if you need to bring a generator. He or she will also check any structure you might want to put a light on (including the ground!) to see if it is strong enough to carry the weight.

3   The DoP will make a lighting plan (a bit like your floor plans), working out and making drawings of where to put the lights.

4   The sound recordist will listen out for any problems you may have. Fridges and ventilation can be switched off when you shoot, but a nearby sports plane airfield will take some work by the production office to deal with.

5   The Art Department will fine-tune their plans and decide on measures to help resolve problems that may occur in other departments, too. They can help the lighting by repainting a room or help camera by building a ramp or a platform.

6   The 1st AD will feed all new information into the schedule to optimise the order in which you will shoot your scenes.

If everything is fine, great — you'll be out of there in ten minutes. If not, any problem that occur will be worked out as you all stand in the same spot, looking at the same reality. A solution made in isolation might work for one department, but it will have a knock on effect on everybody else's arrangements. And there is one variable you can't control and that is something as trivial as the weather.

WHAT DO YOU MEAN 'RAIN'?

Say you were planning to do a scene with a really nice opening crane shot in the garden of a big house. All pretty straightforward. The crane shot is scheduled for 2 o'clock when the light is right. Every time you've been to the location the ground has been rock solid, but last night's rain (the first in three months) has softened it.

Grips tells you the soft ground will not support the crane now, and the weather forecast is more rain over the weekend. Will you have to cancel the crane? The Art Department says they can build a platform for the crane, but will have do it the day before the shoot. Problem solved?

If you're shooting interiors in the morning, then yes. If you're shooting exteriors in the garden, then no. Chances are that the platform will be visible in all your other shots. You can't put the crane anywhere else, so you decide to do the crane shot first thing in the morning (it's always quicker to to move things away than to put them into place).

But hang on… Isn't that the day when the lead actor has been to Paris for his sister's wedding and won't be back until midday? It is. Can we fly them back sooner? No.

You may end swapping whole days around to cater for that crane shot. Just because of a light summer rain the night before.

WOULD YOU BELIEVE IT?

I shot a feature length opening part of a drama series in 2005 where a very big terrorist bomb is detonated during a large international conference. The 'before explosion' location was secured and we found a great place to shoot the 'after explosion' scenes: a newly closed down indoor golf arena. The sloping floor of the huge indoor practice range matched the conference centre perfectly. Locations done and dusted?

On the tech recce three weeks later, someone suggested we skip checking on this location because of time restraints. After some discussion we decided to go there after all and — guess what? When we got there, we discovered that someone had nicked the entire building! Yes, stolen it. You should have seen the faces of the crew! Scrap dealers had stripped away the massive windows, all the cabling and light fittings, handrails and even door handles, to sell on to dodgy builders. All that was left was the skeleton structure. Location gone, in other words. We eventually shot the 'after' sequence in the place we shot the 'before' part, but for a week it was touch and go.

IN SHORT

Assumption is the mother of all disasters. No plan is perfect. You hope for the best but prepare for the worst. The tech recce is when you eliminate what hopefully will be the last outstanding and unforeseen problems. New ones will pop up during the shoot.

Chapter 33 - THE READ THROUGH

Also known as a table read. The read-through is when you gather all the actors, the producer, the scripty and any other crew you would like to be there around a big table and read the script out loud. You should always insist on having one. If more than half of the actors can't be present because of other commitments, it may lose it's value, even if other people are reading in for them. So, plan this well in advance and fix a date as soon as the actors have been cast.

INTRODUCTIONS

It's cool to introduce everybody as you all sit around the table. Many directors take pride in this, even if it is the producer's job. I never do it because I have a problem remembering names and I'm always terrified of what will happen if I do (getting someone's name wrong is a bit of an insult), with potentially devastating consequences for the shoot. So, I play it safe by letting people introduce themselves by saying their name and the name of the character they are playing.

There is an upside to this. If each actor has to introduce themselves, they will have addressed the whole room before it is time to read the script. This can help to defuse any nervousness

NO ACTING REQUIRED

It is important to remember that you want people to just read their parts, not act them. Acting comes later. If they start acting in a way they think the part is to be played, but it is not what you want, they might lose face when the filming starts.

YOU ARE THERE TO LISTEN AND OBSERVE

This is the last time you will experience the whole story played out from beginning to end until the film has been shot and edited. Always have the stage directions read out during the read through, but never, ever do it yourself. You should sit back and listen to the story and visualise it.

You should also pay close attention to what is going on in the room. The actors will be measuring themselves against each other and will give away how they feel about each other, the part, the dialogue and the story. You will learn a lot about them and their personalities just by watching how they interact. Body language says a lot and so do any looks across the table. Attraction? Rivalry? Indifference? It's all information that will be gold dust for when you hit the floor.

The scripty will time the reading, so if there is a noticeable difference in length compared with previous timings you can work out if the actors speaking their lines quicker or slower will make a difference.

AFTER THE READING

When you have finished, say something very encouraging (but avoid making a speech) and listen to the general reactions to the script in the room. If you or your producer picked up on any changes you want to make having heard the reading, tell the scripty straight away. He or she will make notes to be dealt with there and then or later.

Thank everybody individually and answer any questions they might have.

It's getting close now.

Chapter 34 - THE NIGHT BEFORE

I always take the actors out for a drink the night before so they all can meet, get to know each other and start to work out how they interconnect through colleagues they worked with before. Everybody likes a free drink, and it gives you a chance to talk informally about other things than the film. They will disclose little things themselves they weren't going to tell until later just because it's a friendly and informal event.

I'm always the first person to leave. Before I do, I always make a little speech. It lasts for about a minute and in it I make a promise.

THE DIRECTOR'S GIFT

I make my actors a promise: Whatever happens during the shoot, they will always get another take. If they are unhappy about a performance (even if I'm ecstatic about it), all they have to do is to give me a wink or a sign (although I can usually tell anyway) and we'll go for another take straight away — no questions asked.

Some of the best performances I've ever seen came when an actor asked for another take. It has only happened three times in 26 years so that's a one hundred percent hit-rate. But what's the point of the promise?

PRETEND YOU'RE AN ACTOR

Think about it. Imagine you are an actor. (You should be able to do this by now!) You just done the first shot you're in. The director thinks that you were great (or perhaps just grateful that you delivered your lines correctly and no one in the crew screwed up). Still, you have an instinctive, niggling feeling that you could have done it better. That you had more to give. When the 1st AD says 'Let's move on', the moment is gone and your heart sinks. From now on this will come back to haunt you. The first shot you did was not as good as it could have been. Your performance is compromised; you have already been robbed of that extra thing that could have made you a star. Chances are that it will be downhill from here.

The thing is, it rarely takes more than a couple of minutes to do another take of anything if you go straight away without any discussion. If all the actors know they can ask for one more take, they will feel safe. And along with that comes trust. And with trust comes good performances. And with good performances comes a better film. And that is why you are there.

You are the Protector of the Film.

Chapter 35 - FIRST MORNING OF THE SHOOT

You went to bed early last night (don't stay up late to make last minute changes. Trust me when I say you are better off being well rested). You've packed your bag and selected a pair of really comfortable shoes to wear (rule number 1 according to my director friend Simon).

Whatever way you travel to the location, you and your 1st AD should be the first to arrive.

Go through the call sheet with your 1st AD to make sure you haven't forgotten anything. Double check the schedule and talk through the scenes of the day. If you have changed the way you want to shoot a scene since last night, this is the time to share it so the crew can be informed as soon as they arrive. Other things could have happened that you weren't aware of, like an actor's child coming down with the measles, a piece of equipment going missing or someone having started World War III (something you wouldn't have noticed being as nervous as you are).

All directors are nervous on the first day.

You should be. It's a good thing. It's a sign that you care about what you are about to do. If you're not nervous, chances are there's something wrong.

THE FIRST SET-UP

This is it. It's all about to happen. The beast will be unleashed. The moment you've spent endless hours, days, weeks or even months planning for, has finally arrived.

And you wait. And wait. There's nothing more frustrating when you are a director than waiting for the crew to get ready. The first day is always the worst. Your mind is racing but everything around you seems to move soooo slowly. The crew is finding its feet, and if they could, they would spend the better part of day one getting ready. At least that's what it feels like. So here's a good piece of advice:

FIFTEEN MINUTE DEADLINE

Make the first shot of the day something spectacularly simple. The close-up of a door handle or similar. If you don't have a shot that simple, just make one up! No one will ever know if you are going to use it or not, or what it's for. If you can get your first shot done within the first fifteen minutes of the first day, then you will have set up the dynamics for the rest of the shoot.

It might just be the best spent 15 minutes of your career. You will be perceived as a director who gets things done. You will be known as the director who knows what you want. You're off to a flying start and that's how you want things to stay.

So, don't lose your patience. Take a step back and take a moment to look at all the people working away around you and remember what I said in Chapter 1:

Filmmaking is never a mechanical process.
It's when a group of people who learned to trust each other
come together and perform miracles.

Assumption is the mother of all disasters.

Learn to trust your instincts.

*

Before I go, I shall add a fourth point:

Learn from your mistakes.

I've learned so much from my mistakes that I am
thinking about making some more.

Any second now, you will hear your 1st AD shout 'Action!'

But that's another book.

Prep well.

Have fun.

Be good.

APPENDIX I - SHOT SIZES

I refer to various shot sizes in the text. Here's a visual guide to what they all mean:

APPENDIX II

They say it would take us two weeks to cross a road if we couldn't rely on our experience and the things we do automatically. Our brains are beautifully complex, which is why we are the species on the planet that takes the longest to become adults. Here's an example of what happens when the automation doesn't kick in. I was sitting in a hotel room doing my shot plans when I got stuck. To snap out of the mental block, I started writing a list of things you take into consideration when deciding on shots. When I had filled a page I stopped — it became a bit too scary!

FIRST CAMERA POSITION
Or a brief moment of despair

16.00 It;s going well... But slow. In every scene (70 odd per episode) you're trying to be inside the heads and minds of two or more people, simulating the life and experience of characters with a past, at a particular point in the arch of a story, on a day in the future, at a location you've been to maybe twice - where it might rain or where the sun might shine. There are between 3 and 15 beats in a scene, sometimes more. If I start there, where will the camera be at that particular beat? Will the audience instantly recognize where we are? Do I contain it in one or do I "shoot through the lens-box"? Do I track? CAN I track? Do I have time to track? How long can I sustain the first shot? Shall I stay wide or go in close? Are they moving through the whole scene, choreographed, or do they stop? If so, when? And, above all - why? Can I look that way? And if I do, where will the other person be in relation to him and to the car that may be parked there (will it fit between the stone wall and the edge of the road?) - or there (will the motorbike get a clear run through in the scenes before and after?) - and will this create a need for additional angles - or not (carrying the same questions)? If I DO use that part of the location, will it look as if we're somewhere else, since that pine tree is uncharacteristic and cannot be seen from any other angle I'm using in this scene? What if... He's over there - then the car has to be there... How do I jump them from there from there in a seamless way so I'm at point A when I'm at beat X in the script? Does it matter? Can I keep some of the dialogue out-of- shot to bridge the gap? Is the jump too far for the location? Do I see/make enough use of the location/landscape or could I have shot this at the studio? Is it a bonus to see that view again, will it create resonance or will it just be repetitive? Are we under/over informing? Is it distracting at that particular point? Is it too simple and conventional - or too contrived? Does it look lazy or indulgent ("oh, they couldn't be bothered to move the camera/they liked the shot so much that they did it again...) Has this shot been done before? Will the viewer be captured by this moment? Will it inspire the cast? Will it keep them out in the rain? If it doesn't, what's my simplified version, or if I run out of time - how do I cover all the beats in 1 fixed, static setup - and still keep the integrity of the script, the characters, my style, my ambition...? Will I be proud of this? "Jonas, what's my motivation to take that step to the left? "Jonas, are you aware of the noise from the stream over there?" "Can't get around that camera shadow" There might be a gale, the actor might have a bad day, the place could be flooded... ("let's do it over there instead...!") The possibilities and restrictions are endless and overwhelming... Every beat is important. No chain is stronger... etc. Playing scenes backwards and forwards so many times in my head, just to find the one fixed point for the way in. Sometimes it feels as if your head is going to explode, you keep putting scenes away for a while and come back to them again, later. And again... That little extra in every scene makes a huge difference for the whole. Every character is the Star of every given moment they're in, because they're the ones who the audience watch - not me... And yet, it's not "Gone with the wind". It will never be fully satisfactory, and 15 seconds later it's "yesterdays newspaper..."

JG September 2002

APPENDIX III - ACKNOWLEDGEMENTS

This is by far the trickiest part of this book. You can never thank everybody. If I did, there would be thousands of names here; listing them all would double the page count. It is, however, necessary to single out a few.

Thank you Janos Hersko, Krystyna Lesniewska, Elisabeth Lee, Olle Unnerstad, Madeleine von Heland and Dick Ross, who educated me at Dramatiska Institutet and the Royal College of Art. Thanks to my friends Sophie Dow, Simon Shore and Dick & Phyllis Ross again for their support throughout my career.

Thank you to all the casts and crews I worked with over the years. Thank you to producers Astrid Ohlsén, John Davies & Jill Neville, Andrea Calderwood, Christian Wikander, Stefan Baron, Scott Meak, Gerry Mill and, above all, Archie Tait, who came up with the idea of me holding the seminar at the London Film School which was the starting point for this project. If he hadn't, this book would never have been written. I remember telling him yes, I could talk about how a director prepares for half a day and seeing him looking back at me with a smile and say 'No Jonas, it will be a two day event.' I burst into a sweat. This book is the essence of that seminar. It's the same but different (I'm not using any film clips here), and above all it is more condensed. In writing you can be more economical.

Thank you to Tabitha Jenkins, Jonathan Taylor and Andrew Sanderson for helping me and approving of my description of what you actually do; Dominic Clemence for involving me in a never-ending conversation about life and film making; and Tiarnan O'Sullivan, Michael Boccalini, Antony Alleyne and Zsofi Debreceni for being part of the reader's group. Thank you Eleanor Marriot and Elisabet Baldwin for proofreading the manuscript and, by doing so, improving it exponentially. Thank you to Anglo-Swedish Society and the supporters of the Kickstarter campaign who helped financing the printing of this book. Thank you Åsa Höjer for the beautiful design and layout. My muse and Katharina List for giving me the idea to write the book, and finally, my daughter, Ellen, for being my raison-d'etre.

*

That will do for now. Stop reading, go out making films!
Jonas Grimås
London 20 October 2014

CONTRIBUTORS WHO PLEDGED TO HAVE THEIR NAME PRINTED IN THE BOOK

Archie Tait

Thomas Almesjö
Stephen Chambers
Sophie Dow
Carina Einarson
Anders Tobias Falk
Jan von Heland
Anders Lenhoff
Urban Renström

Ria Danielsson
Annika Goodwille
Sofie Marin Haag
Gabriel MacArtney
Gordon Peaston
Isabel Catalán Sada
Haakam Singh
Mohamed El Sehrawy
Janey Walklin

Monica Agorelius
David Anderson
Carolyn Atherton
Mary Benham
Erica Bergsmeds
Indra Bhose
Nigel Bristow
Michael Brolin
Simon David Eden
Lauren Davis
Malin B Erikson
Ellis Freeman

Bibi Fricotin
Bodil Larsson Frånlund
Christer Frånlund
Ellen Sofia Grimas
Alexander de Habsbourg
Lotus Hannon
Hayley Holbrook
Elisa Cherene Holliday
Lotta Hovhammar
Jörgen Jonsson
P-G Jönsson
Rebecca Knapp
Andreas Lindström
Malin Lundén Schmid
Nicola Mathers
Rose McGinley-Redón
Alexandra Metaxa
Jose Nieuwstad & Kew Lin
Pelle Norén
Michal Obuchowski
Bo Olofsson
David Pearson
Siobhan Pemberton
Michael Persson
Sara Pertmann
Palesa Rasekoala
Krysten Resnick
David Sellwood
Heikki Simppula
Anna Södergård
Edward Thomas
Rupert Ward-Lewis
Fredrik Wetterhall
Tim Wybrow